QUADRANT FANTASY

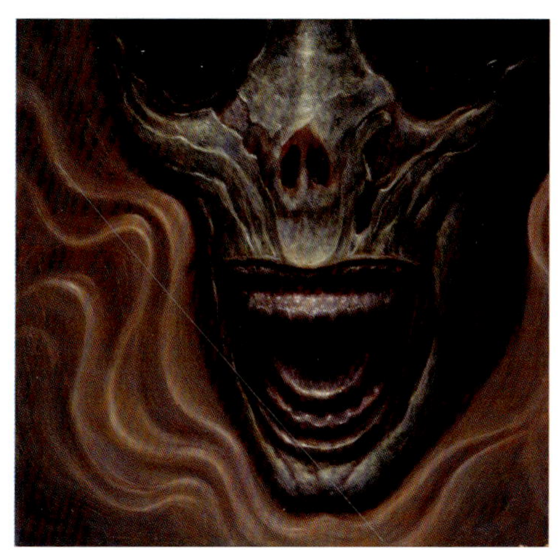

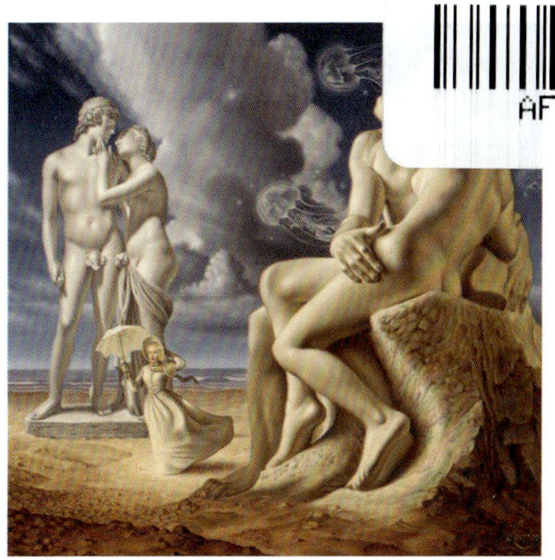

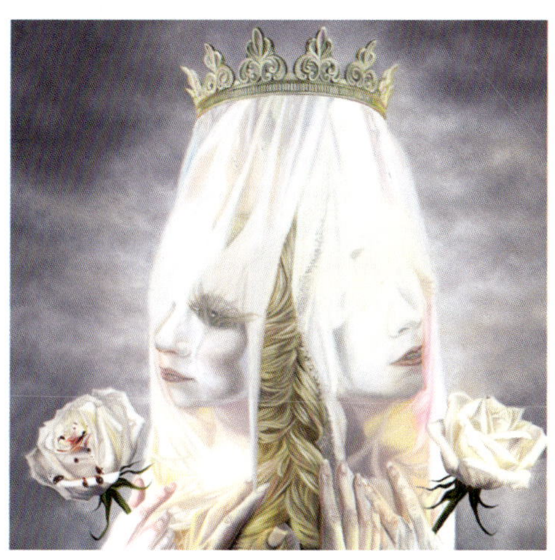

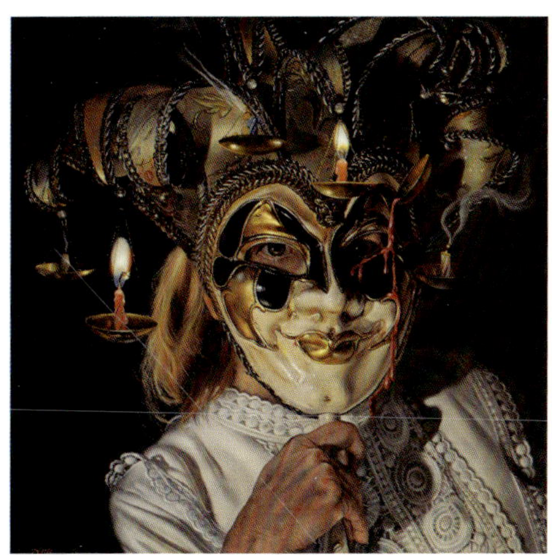

QUADRANT FANTASY

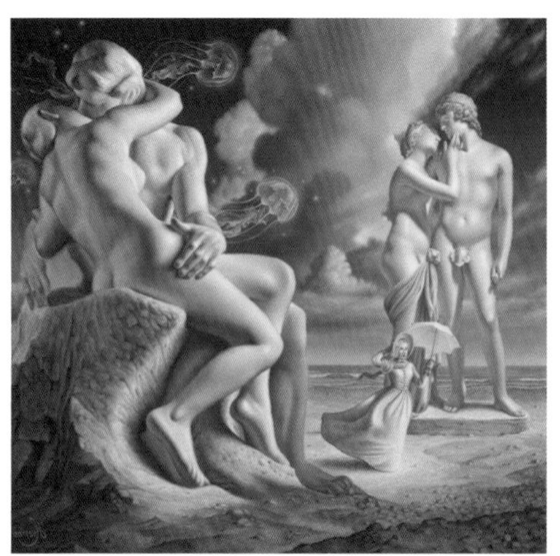

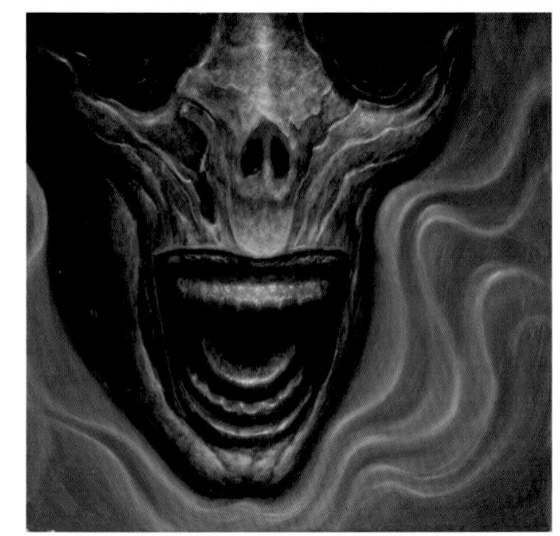

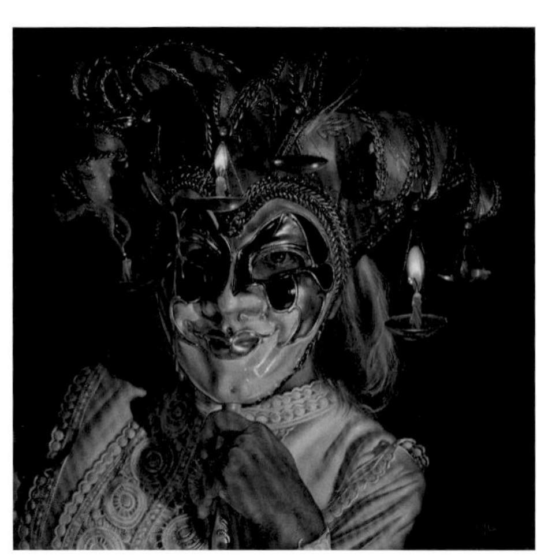

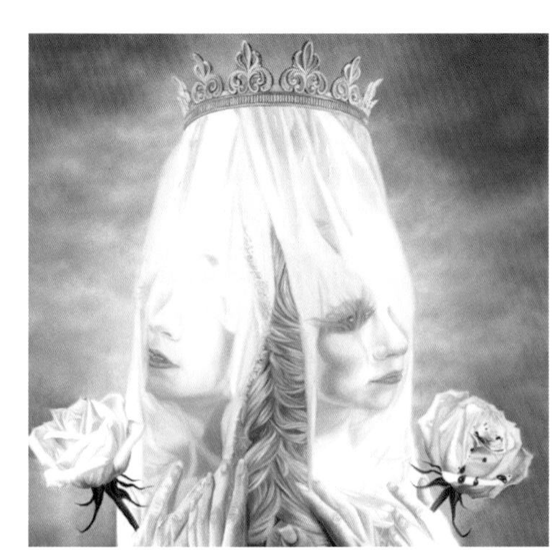

FANTASMUS
&
STRYCHNIN GALLERY

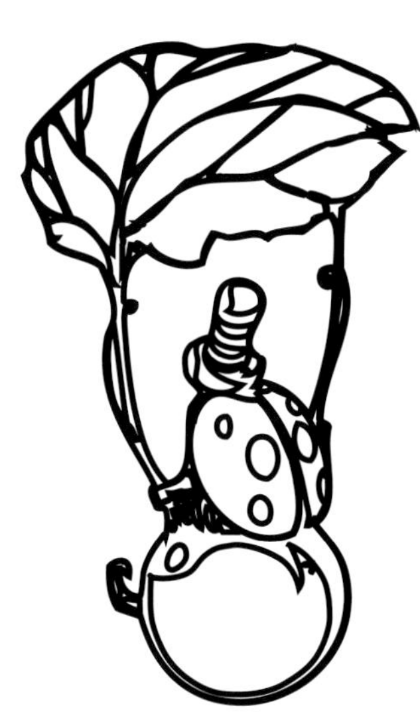

QUADRANT FANTASY

INDEX

INTRODUCTION

In the seventies and beginning of the eighties, music and art combined in the field we today call MAGIC REALISM / GOTHIC ART. Those were the days when buying a new album was a true adventure, putting on this album and study the cover at the same time, gave the full sense of enjoyment.
Today this cooperation is gaining more and more interest, and has actually always done so in Progressive Rock, though many thought it would die out with the coming of the CD. In order to keep the tradition alive, the music industry produced special editions which included more work of an artist, which made these objects into collectors items.
It is truly a great pleasure to bring together an exhibition where the format of the works (except some sculptural art) is the same as the old Record sleeves - a trip back to the times before CDs and IPODs. It is also a great pleasure to have among us some of those artists who made history with their cover art, such as
MARK WILKINSON, DAVID STOUPAKIS & PATRICK WOODROFFE,
just to mention a few.
This exhibition was not born with the idea of making a tribute to the old vinyl album covers, but since so many of those participating were in the business of working for music as a part of their creative force, this was obvious.
This is also the first time I have curated an exhibition in cooperation with another gallery, and it is very exciting to work alongside STRYCHNIN GALLERY. The artists chosen by STRYCHNIN GALLERY come from varied backgrounds in art, such as low-brow, pop surrealism and gothic, and will help to excite and intrigue the visitors of this exhibition. Along with many sculptures, this will also be the first time photography will be displayed at FANTASMUS.
But we must not forget that this is first of all an exhibition of art, and therefore it is about all those fine artists who have agreed to take part, the fifth Easter exhibition at the Center for Art of International Imaginary Realism under the name FANTASMUS.

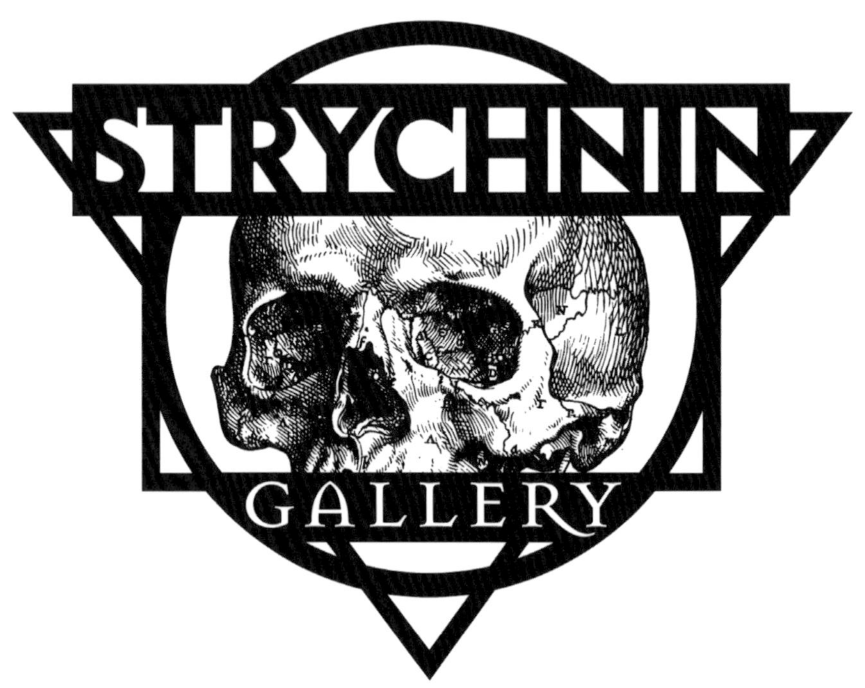
STRYCHNIN
GALLERY

Katarina Ali · Serbia

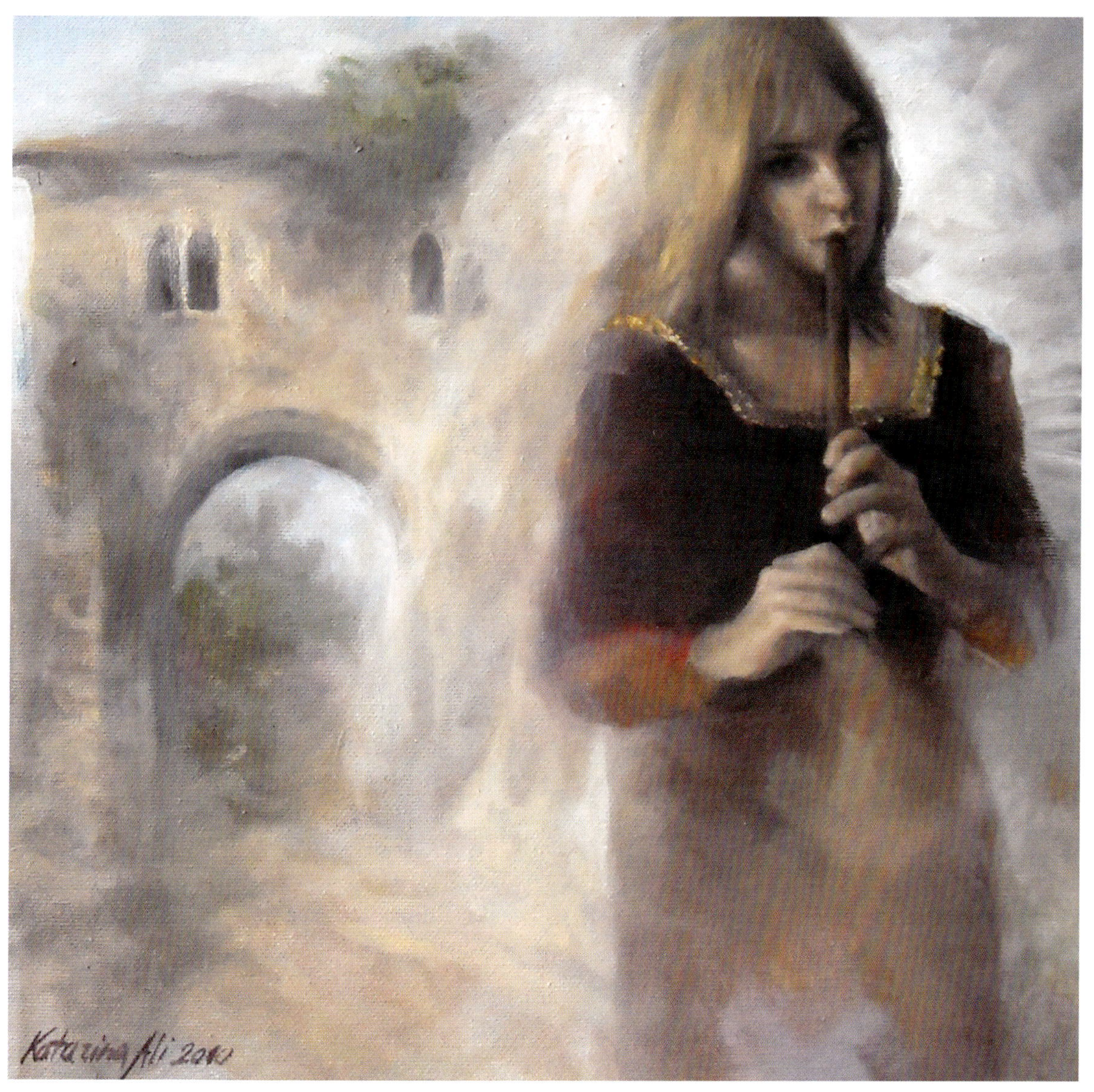

Angels Aura · *oil on canvas*

Annie Bertram · Germany

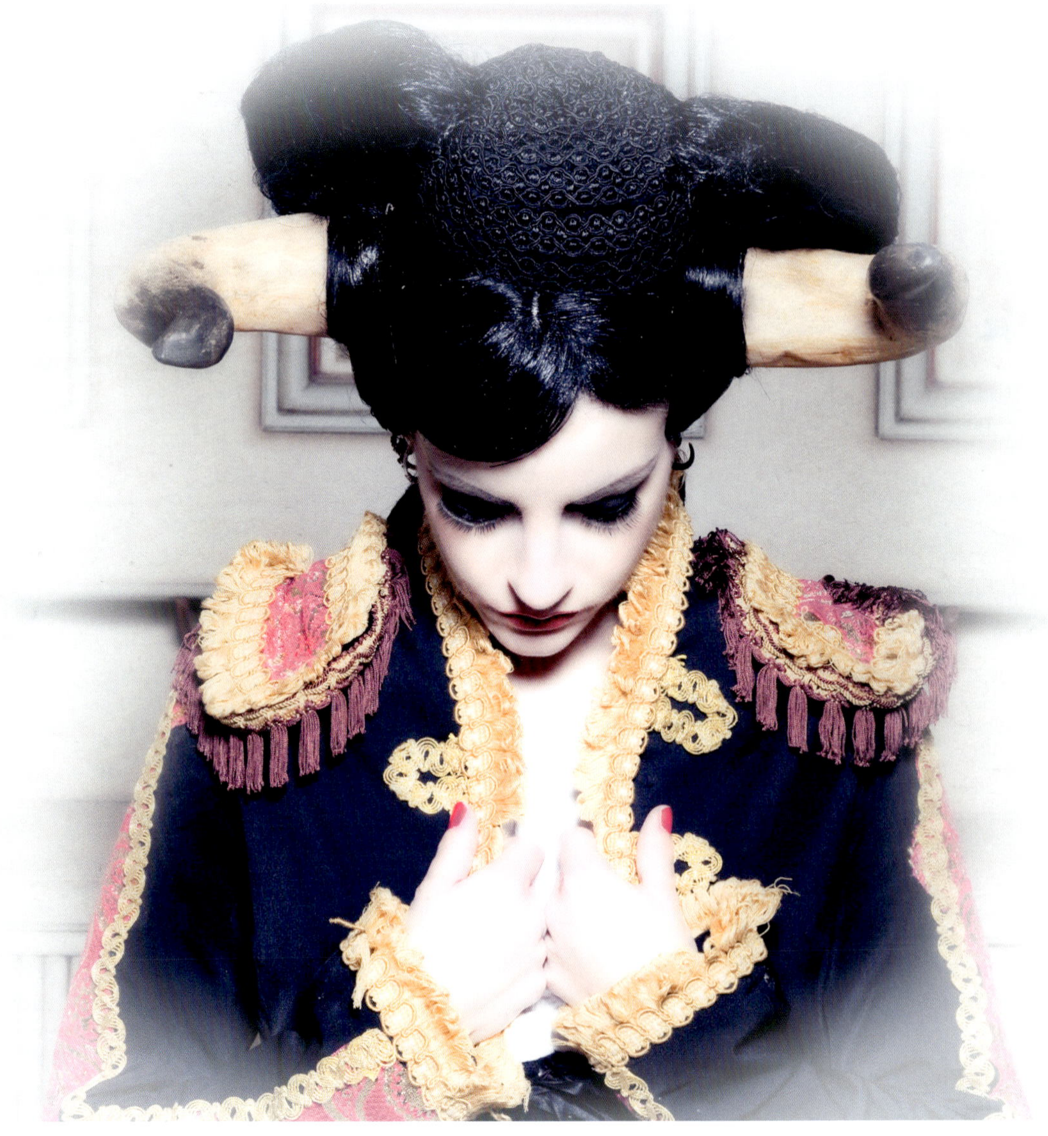

Matador · *photography*

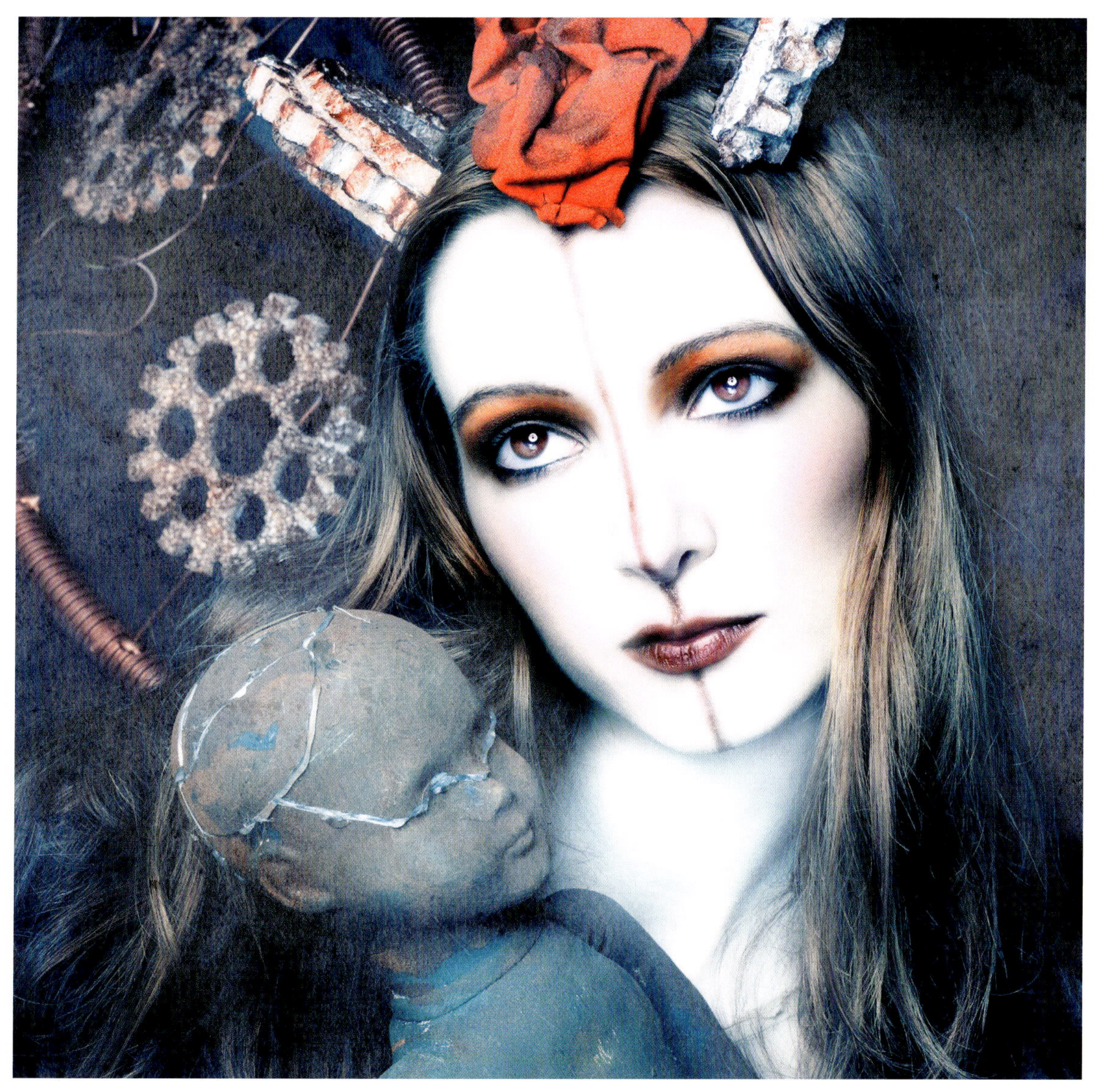

Rusty · *photography*

David M. Bowers · USA

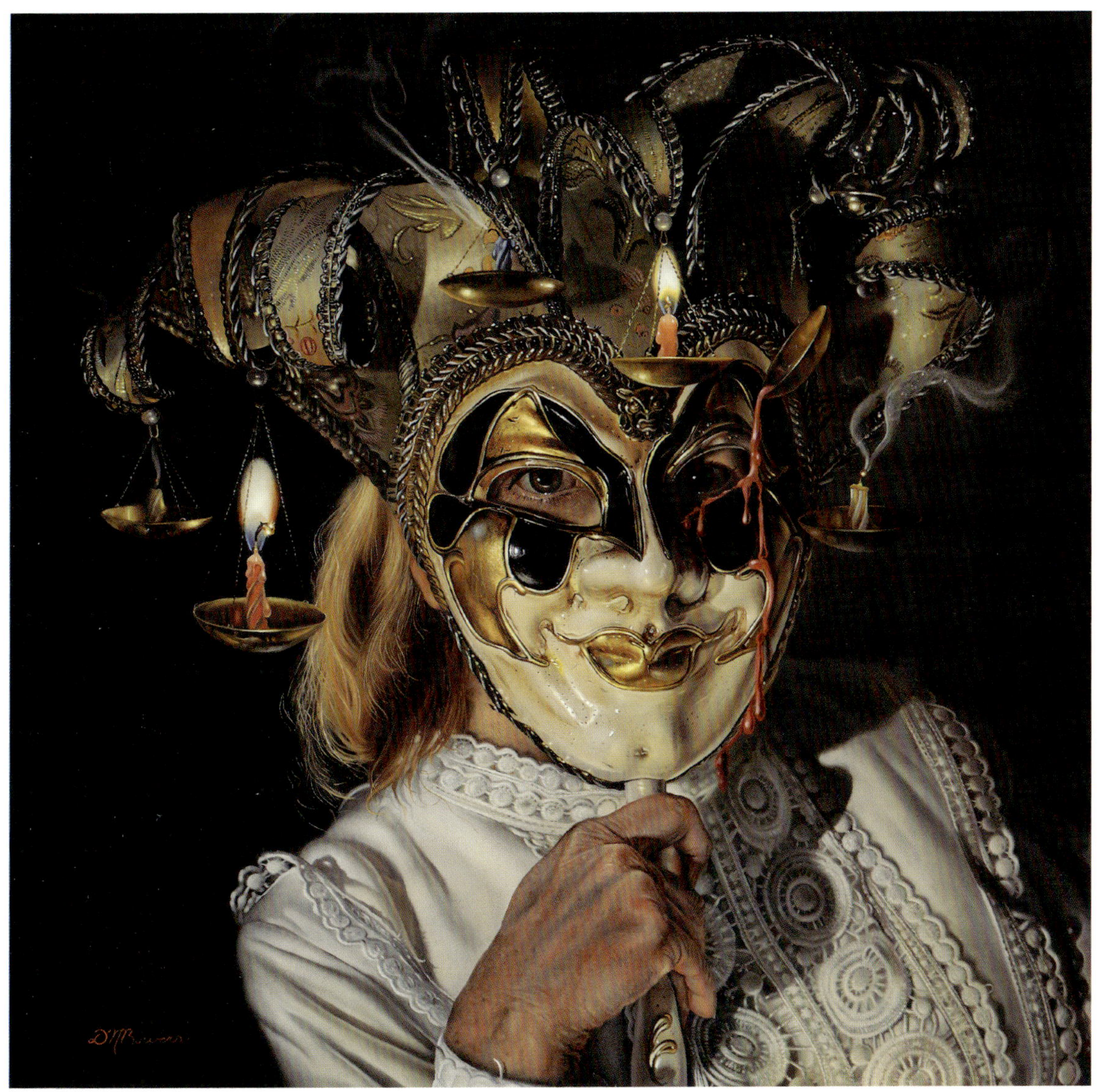

The Wish · *oil on hardboard*

Claus Brusen · Denmark

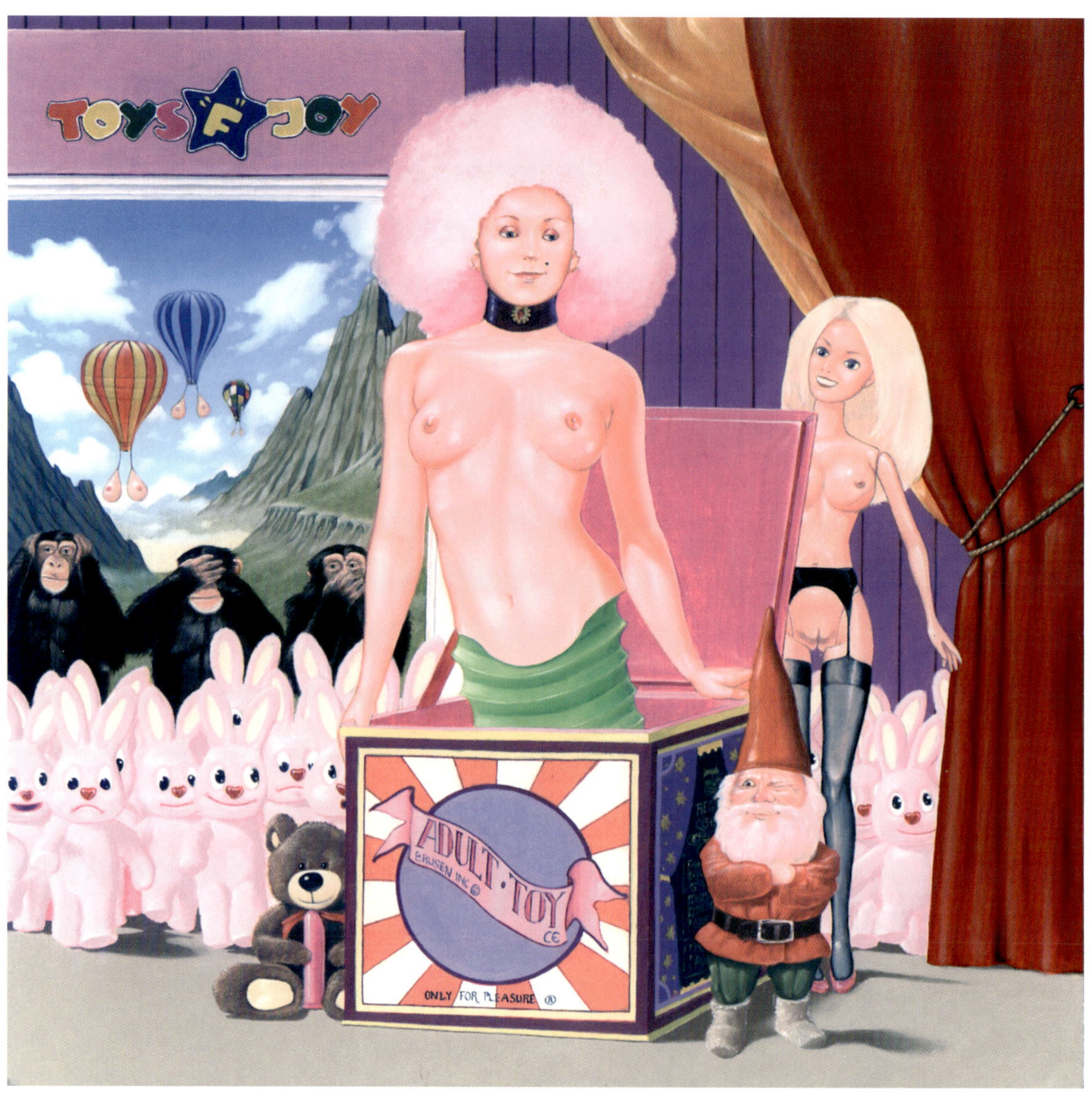

Adult Toy · *oil on panel*

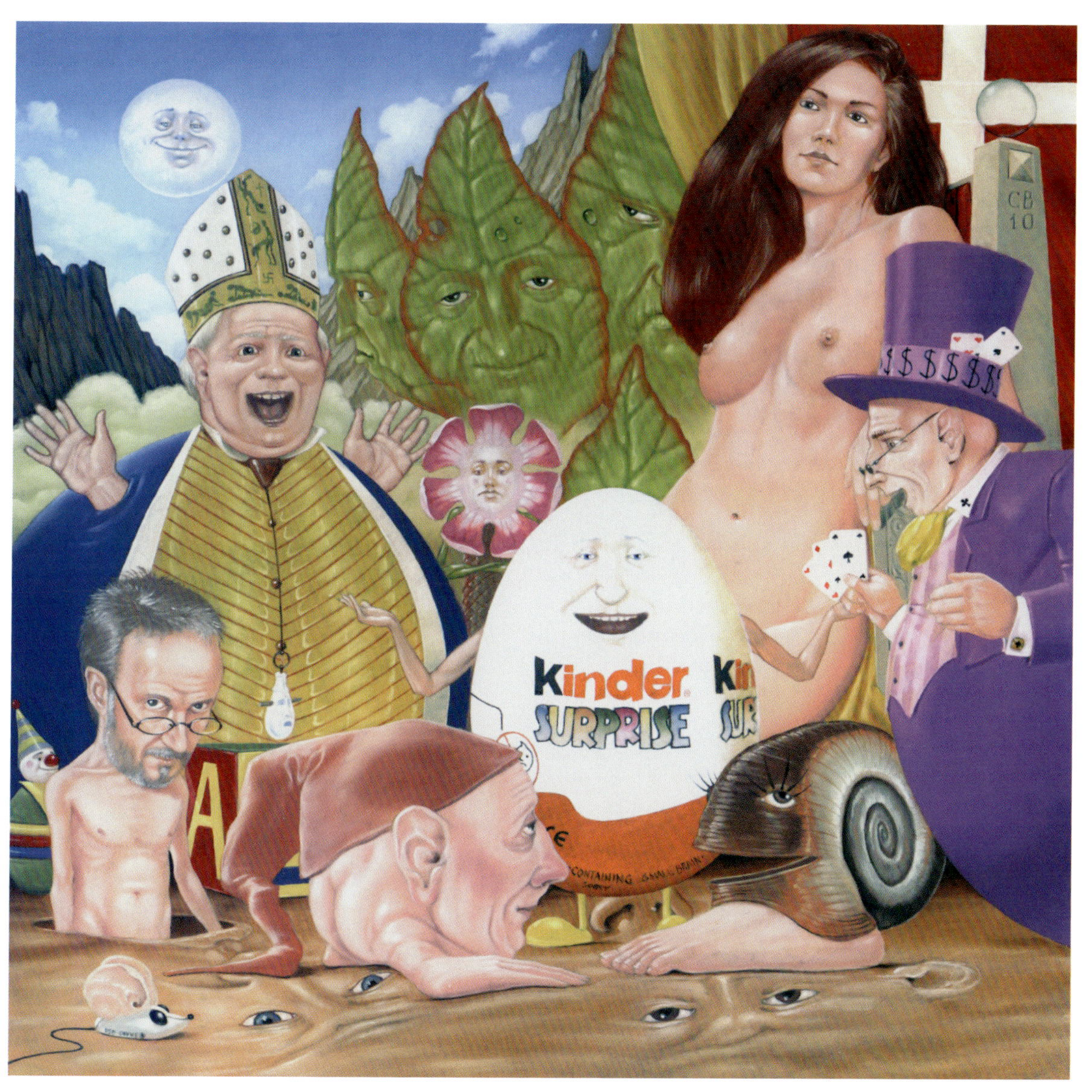

Kinder Surprise ? · *oil on panel*

Gil Bruvel · USA

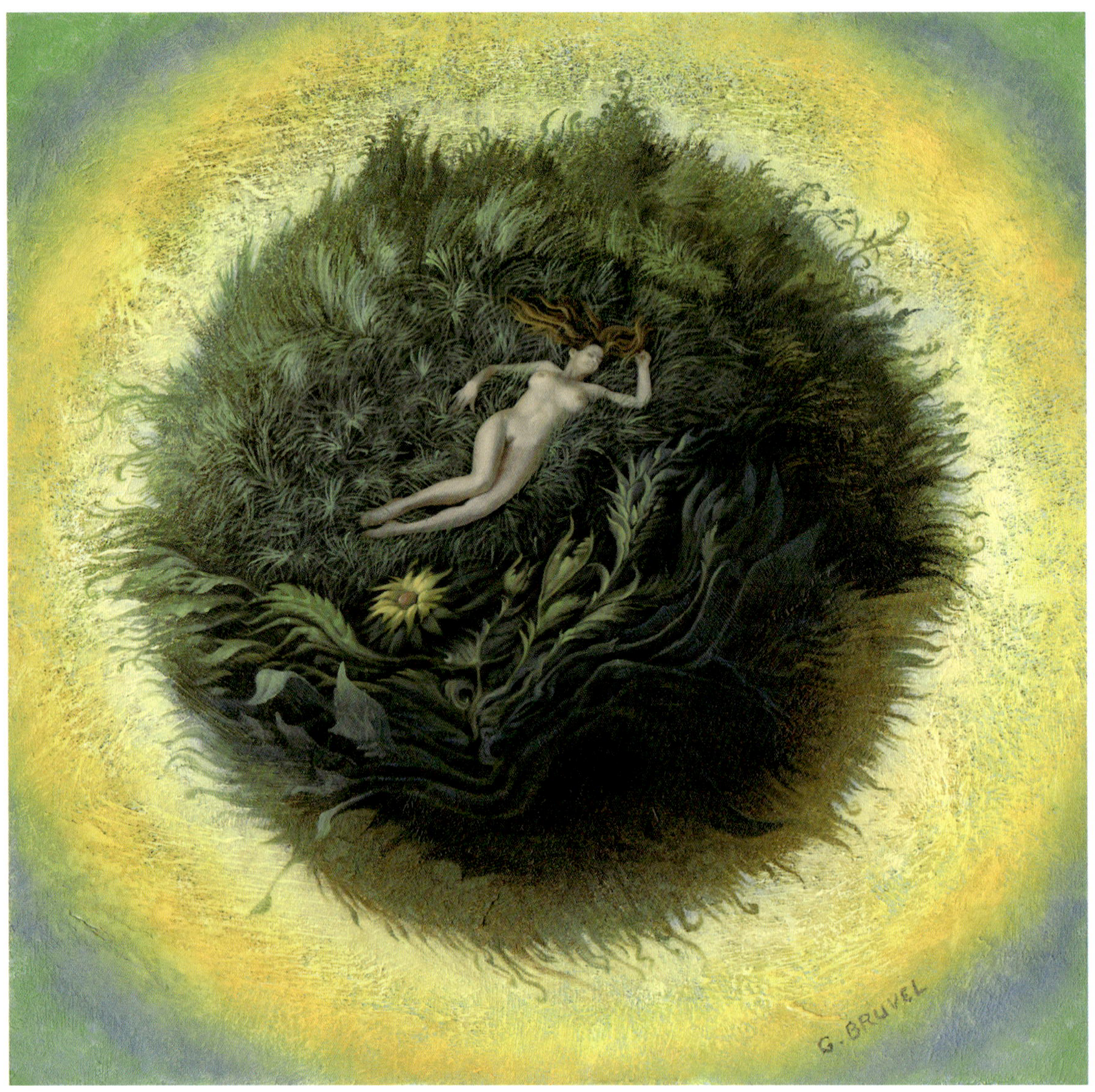

The Refuge · *oil on panel*

Michael Cheval · USA

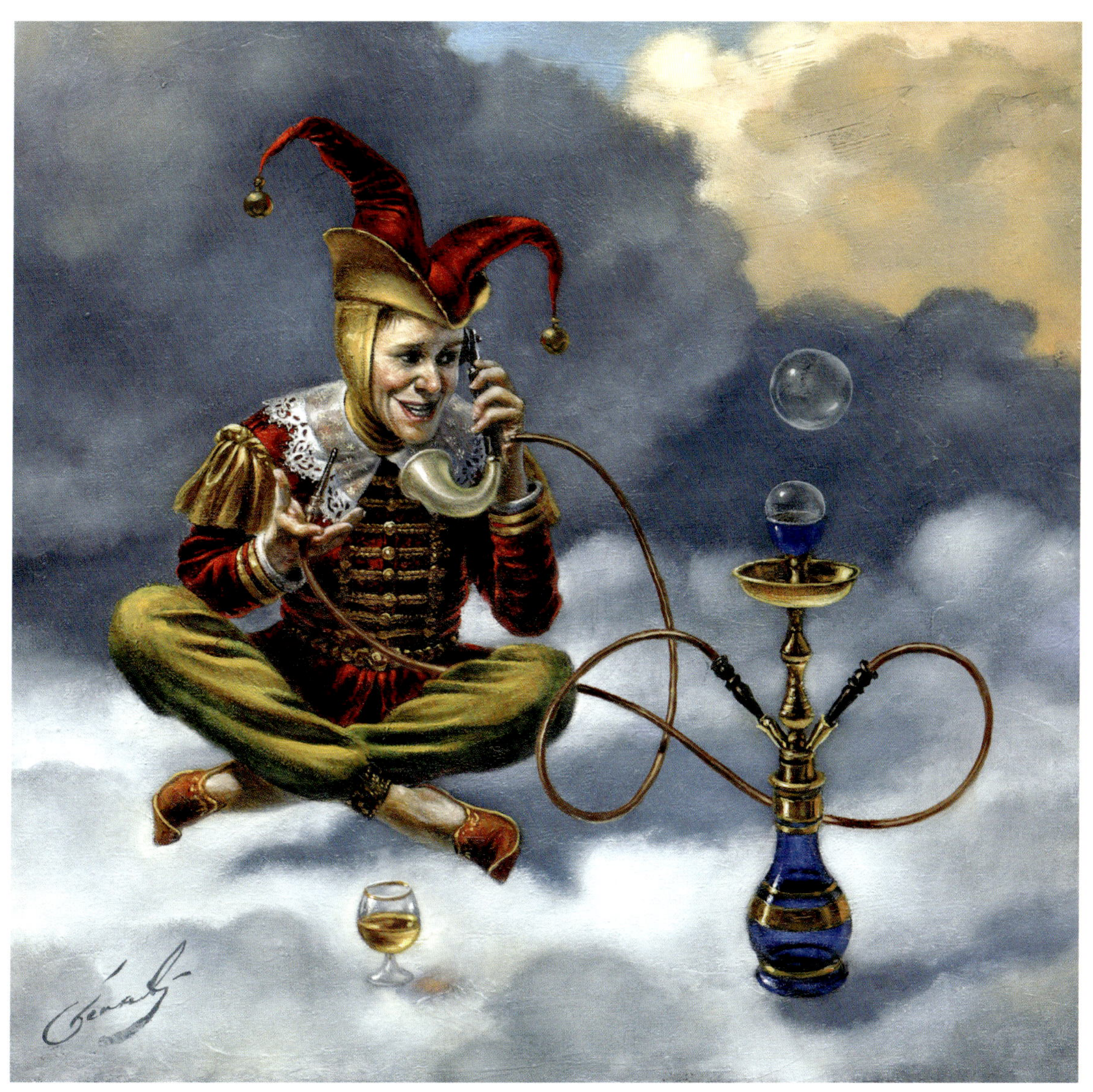

Local Call · *oil on canvas*

Val Dyshlov · USA

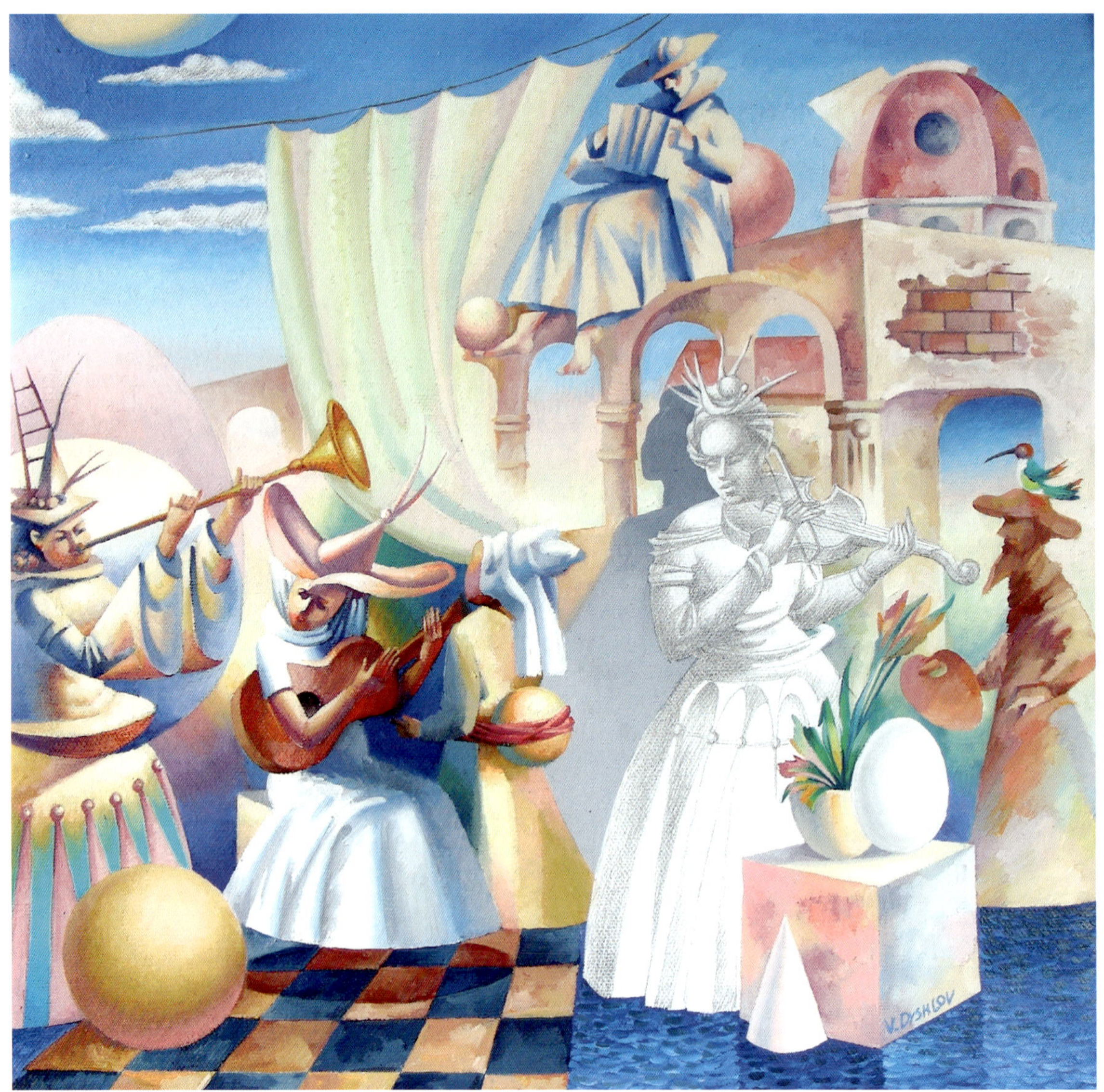

Street Band · *oil on canvas*

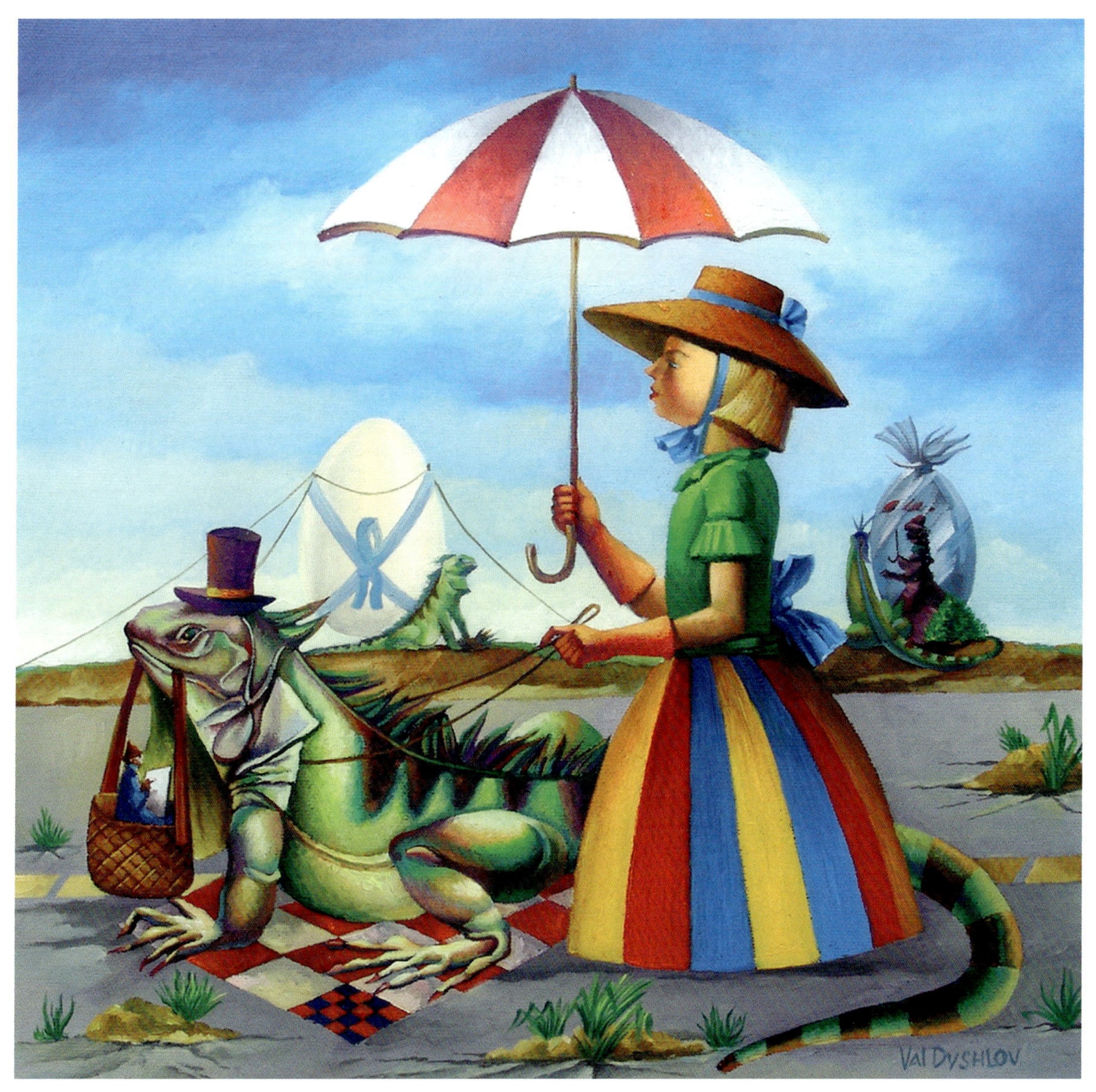

The Walk · *oil on canvas*

Francois Escalmel · Canada

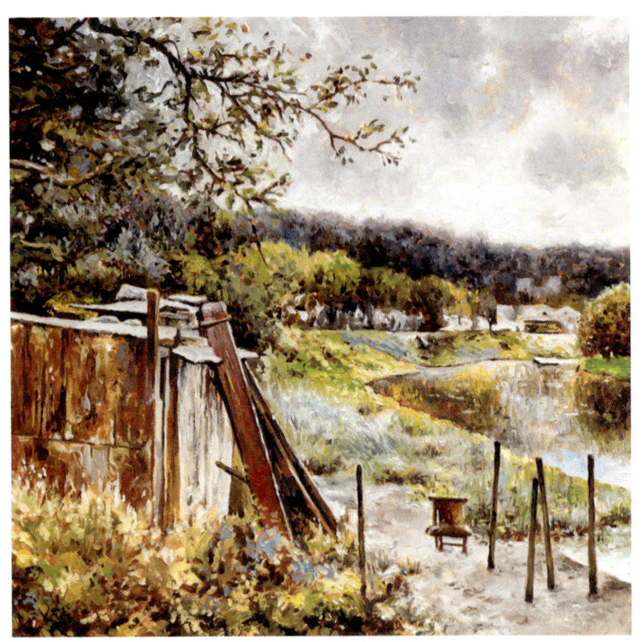

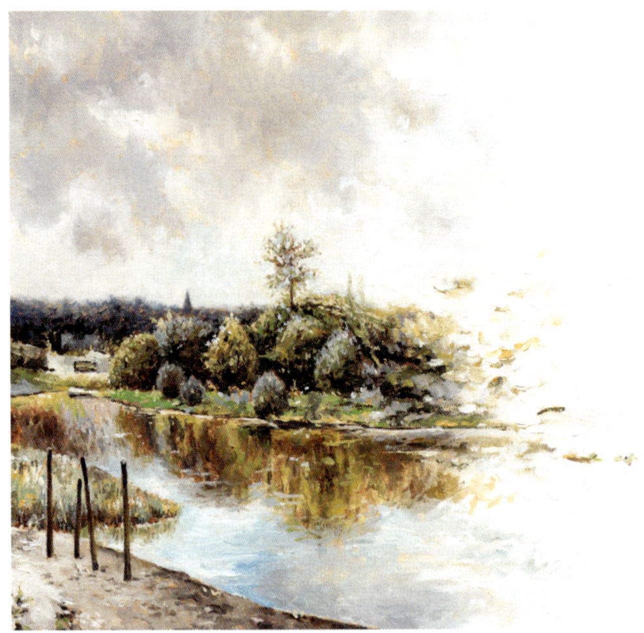

Freight Train Blues · *oil on canvas "Series of 4."*

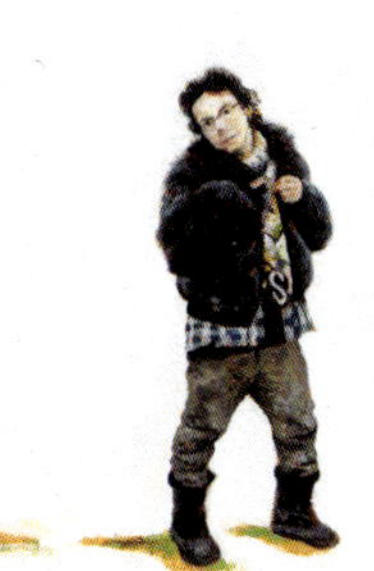

Magda Francot · Belgium

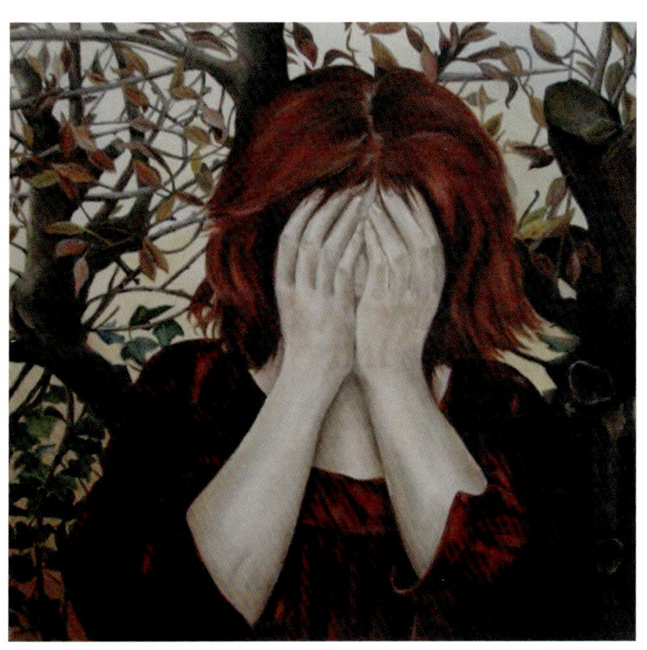

See Nothing · *oil on panel*

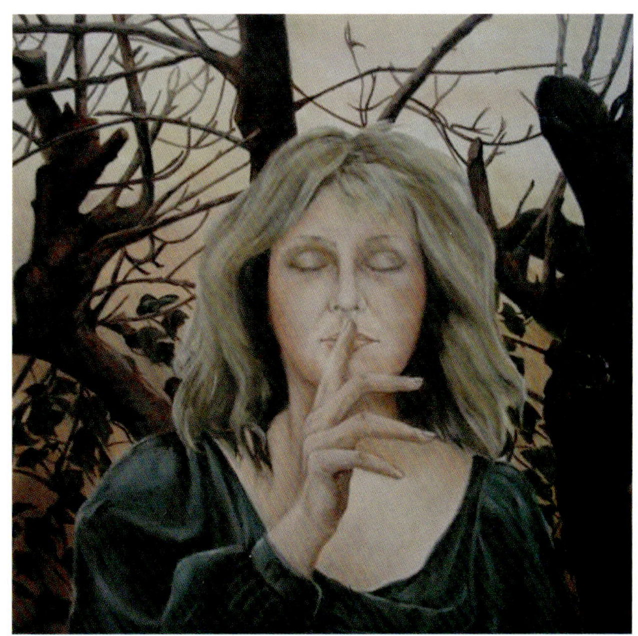

Say Nothing · *oil on panel*

Andreas N. Franz · Germany

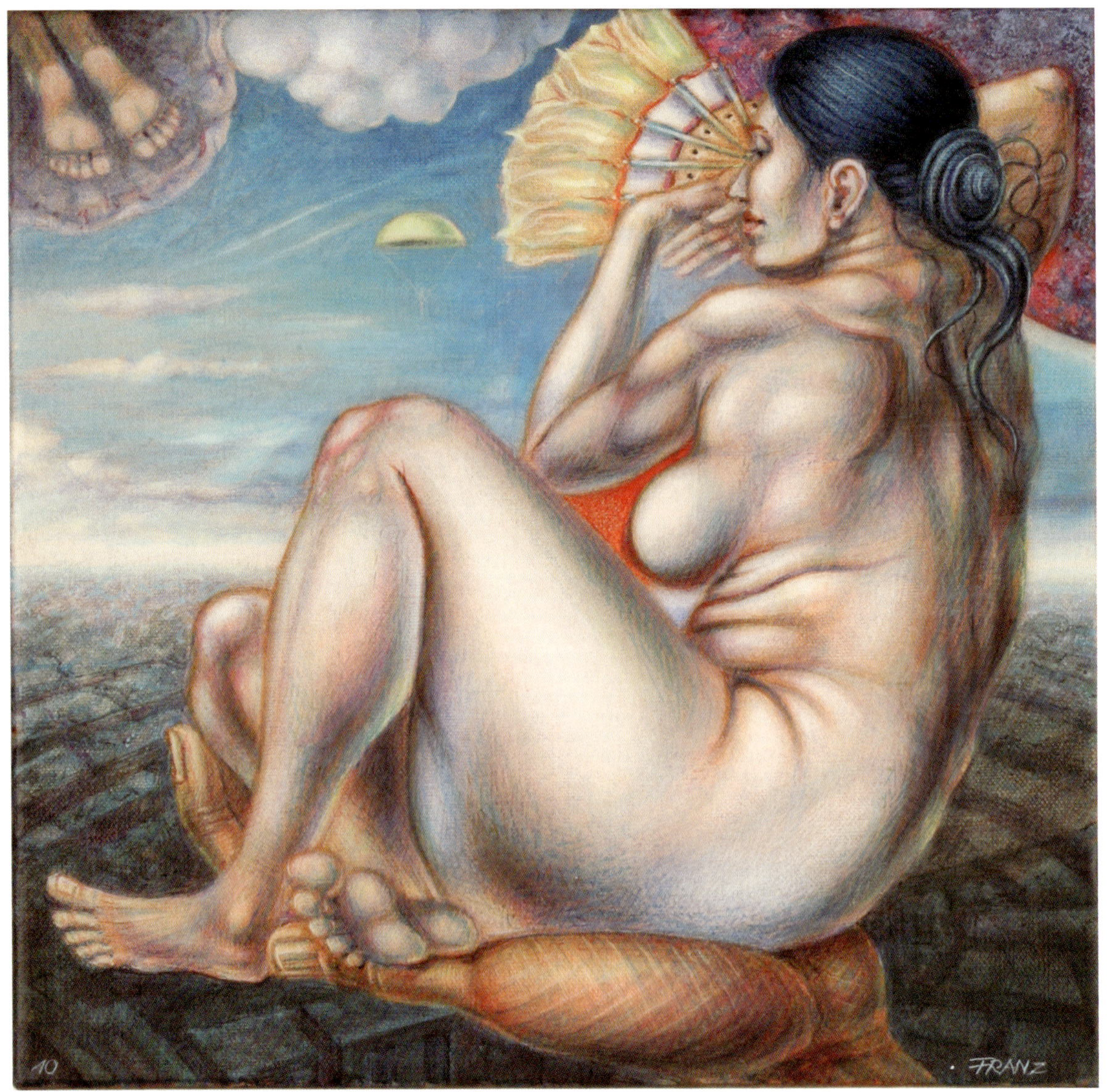

Emotion · *oil on panel*

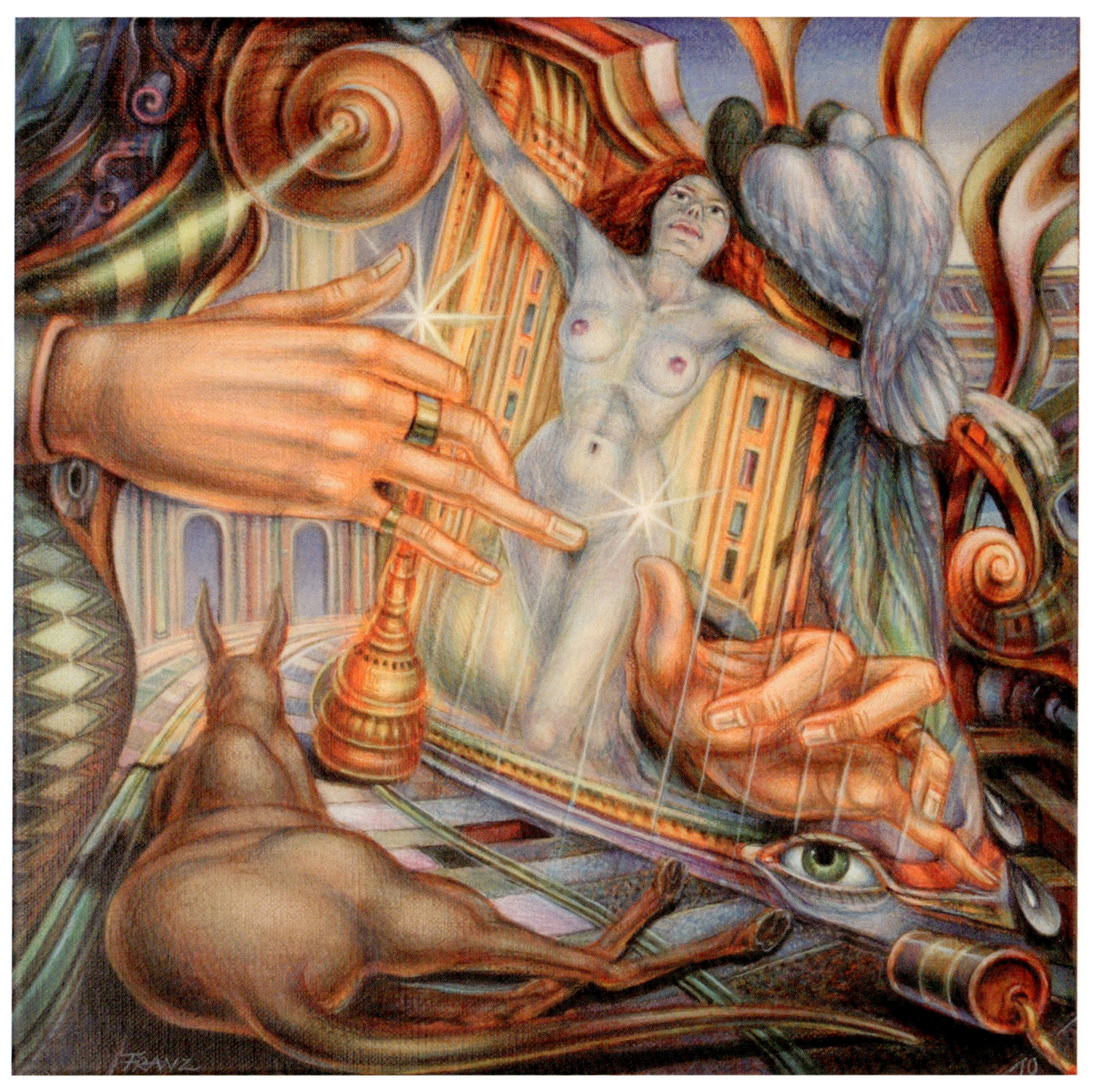

Resonance · *oil on panel*

Kaelen Green · USA

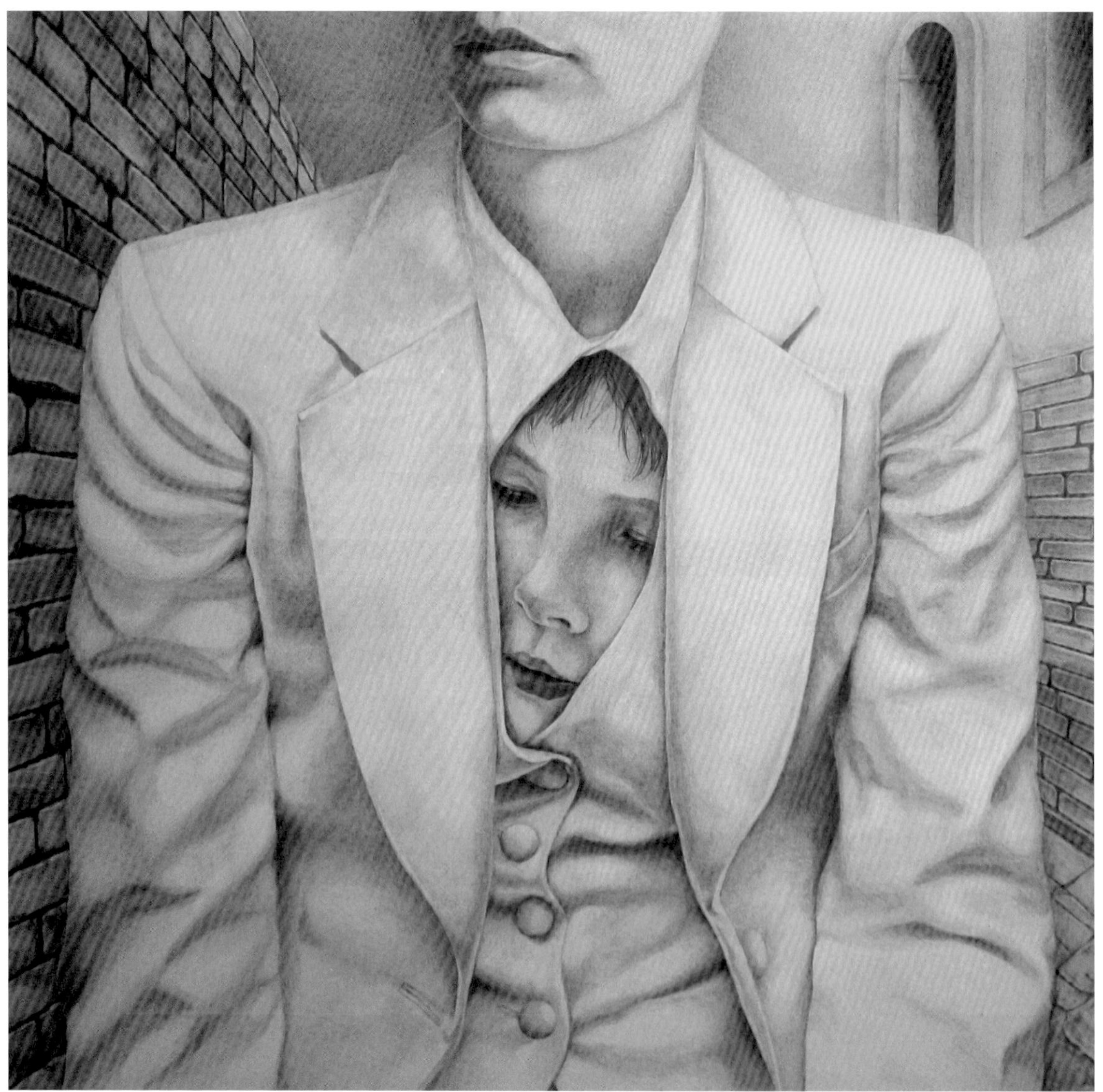

The Here and Known · *graphite on paper*

Linda Groen · Netherlands

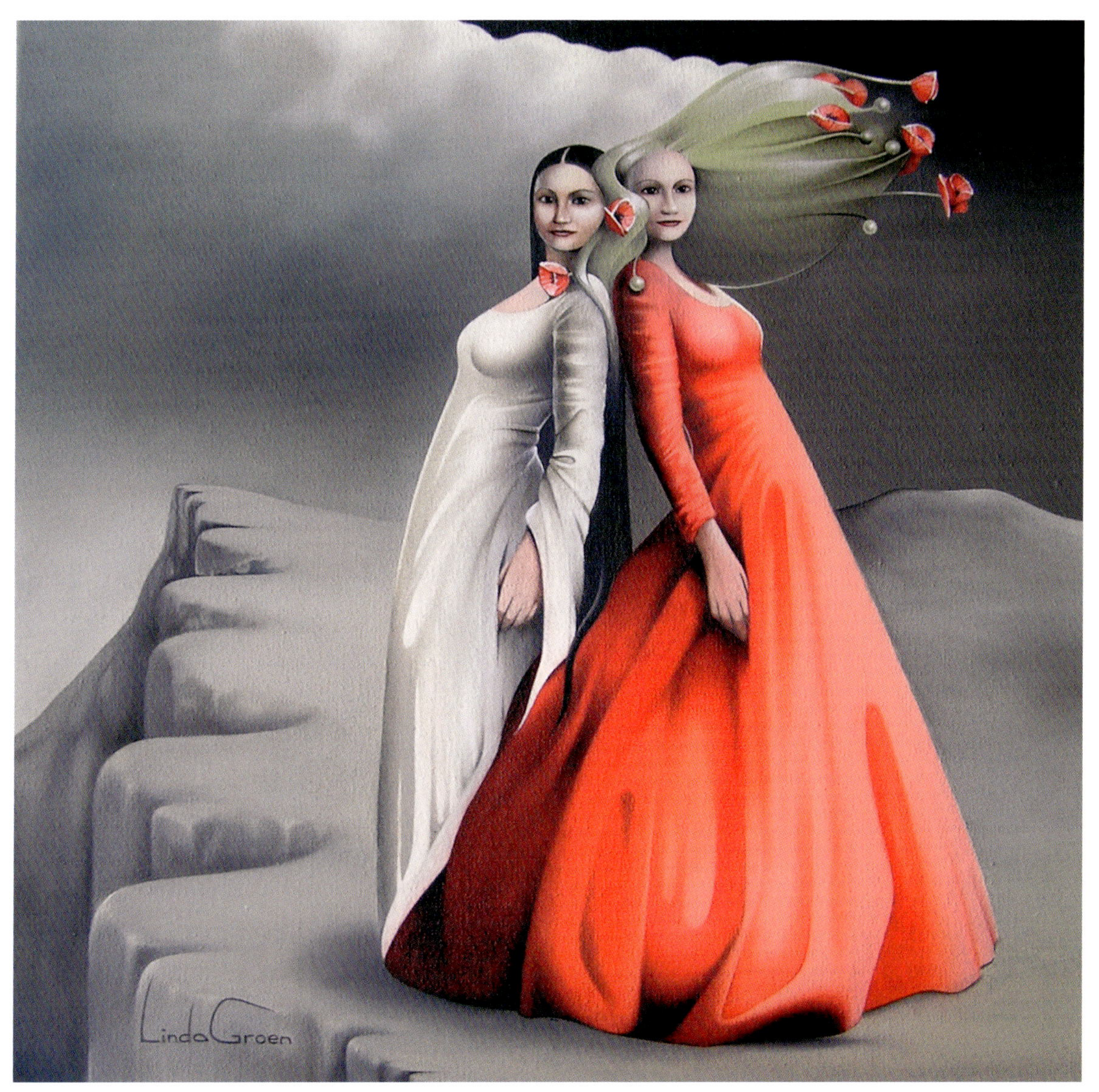

We love him · *oil on canvas*

Gene Guynn · USA

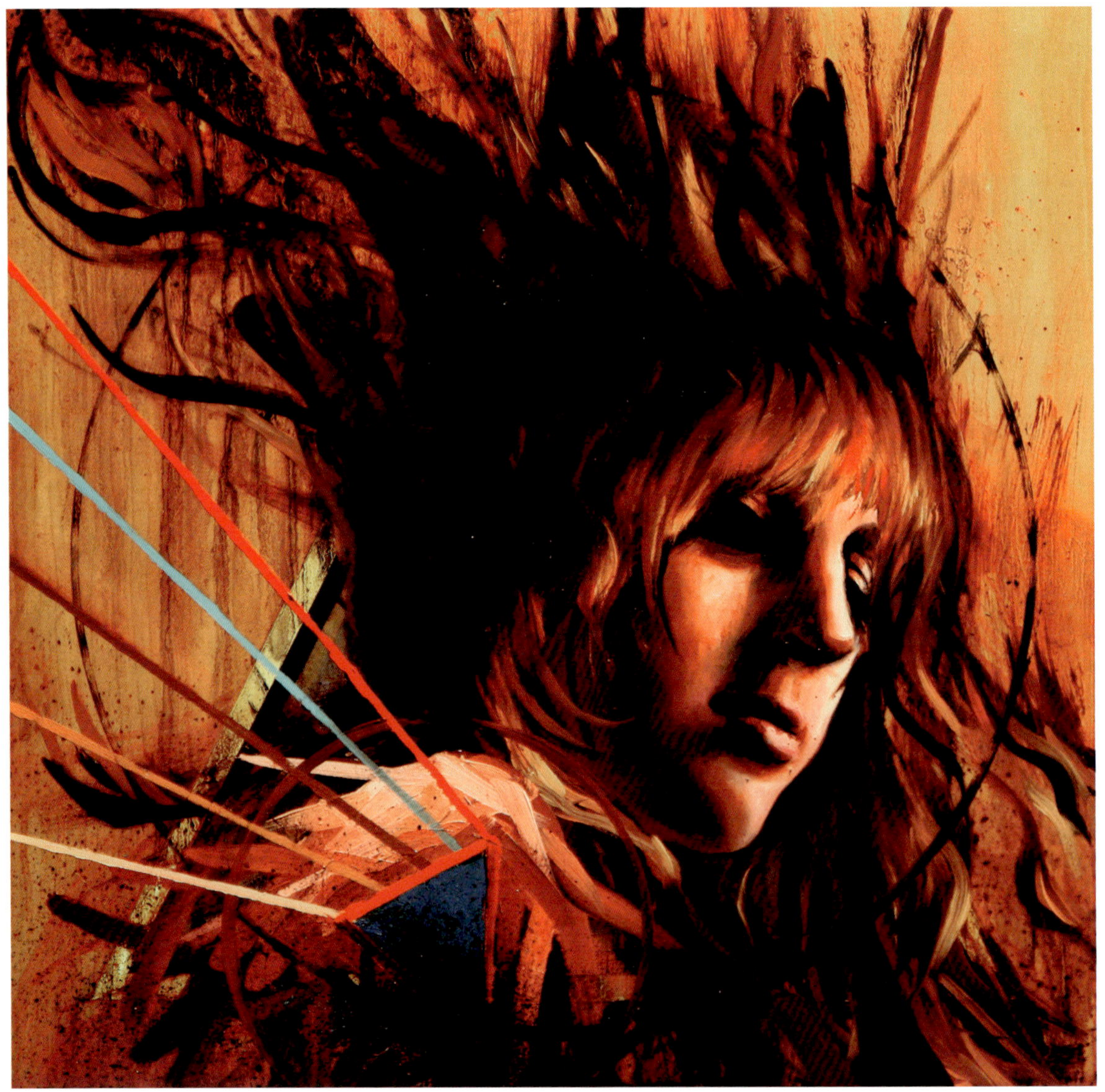

Arachne · *oil, spray paint & Charcoal on panel*

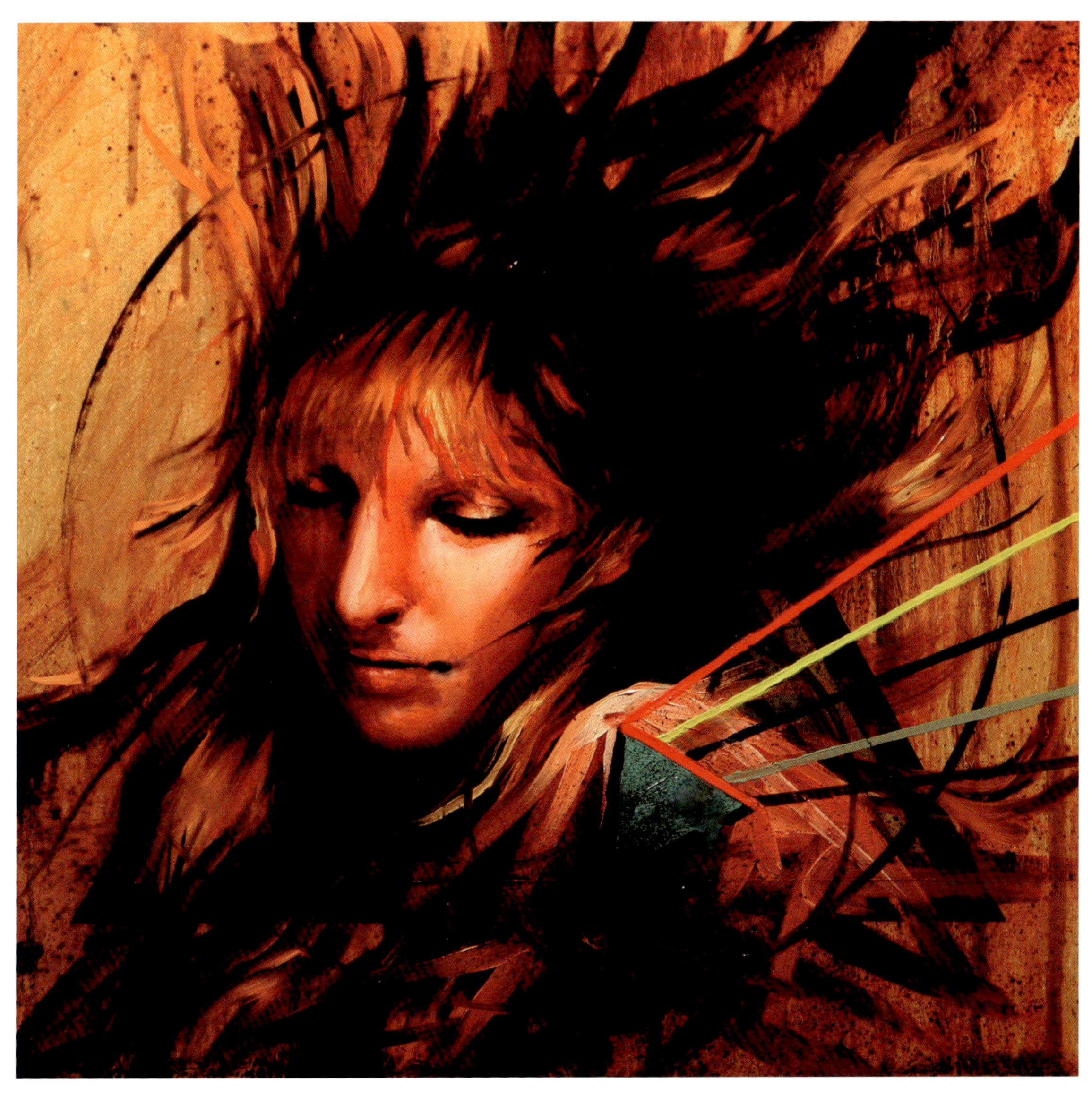

Discordia · *oil, spray paint & Charcoal on panel*

Michael Hiep · Netherlands

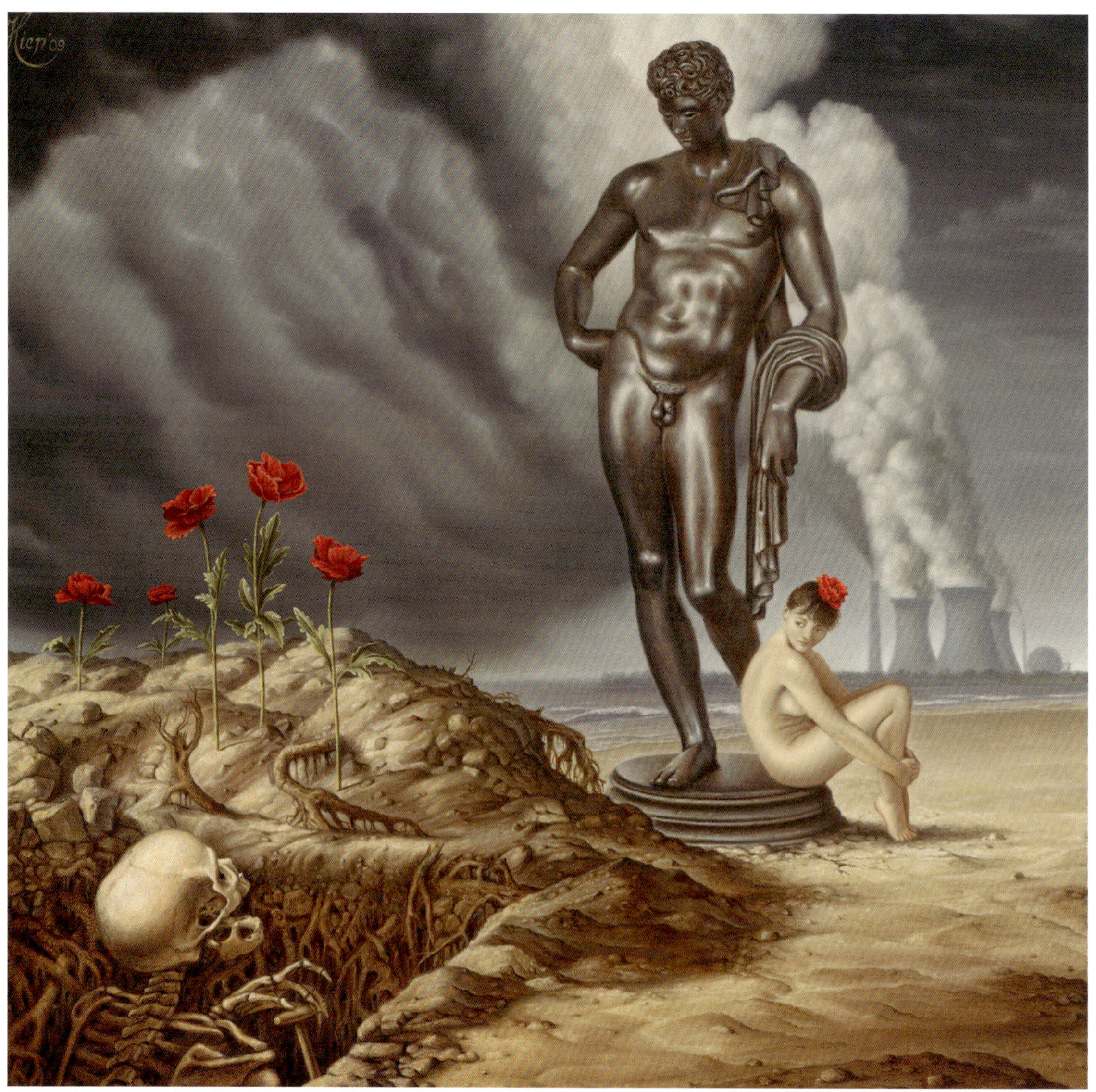

The Excavation · *olie på plade*

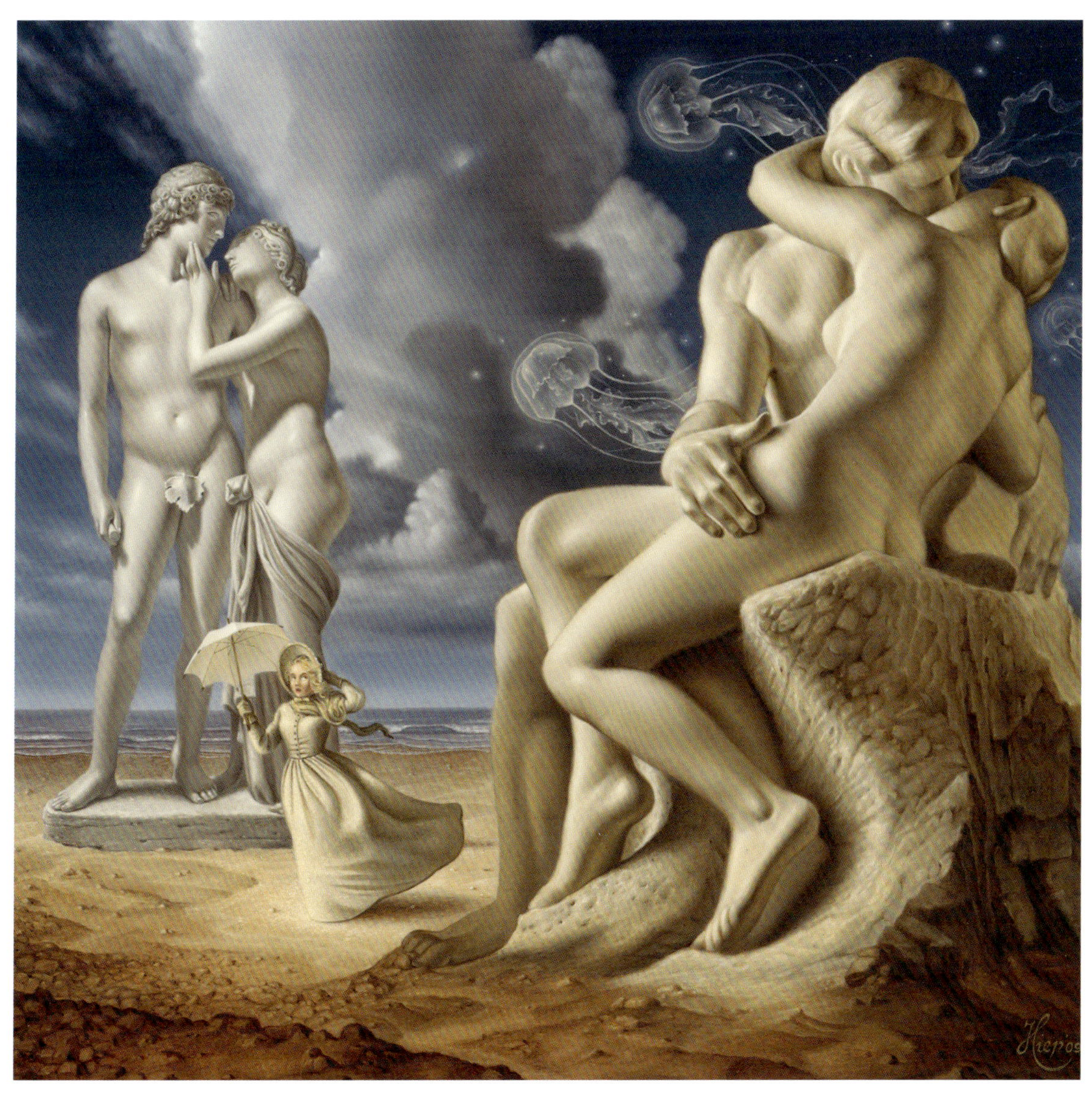

The Nightmare of the White Widdow · *olie på plade*

David Hochbaum · USA

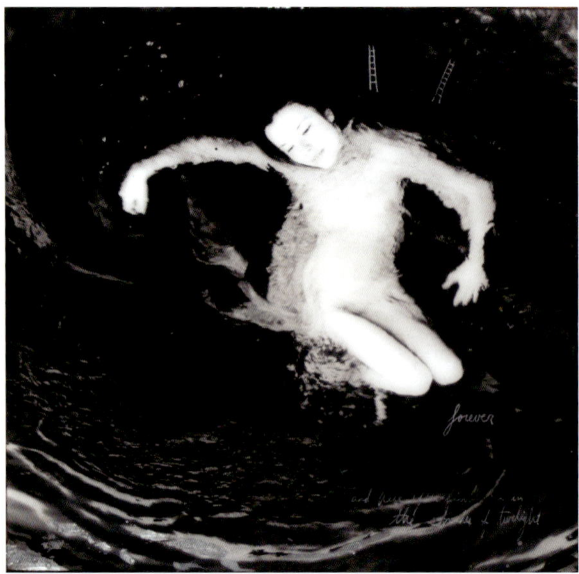

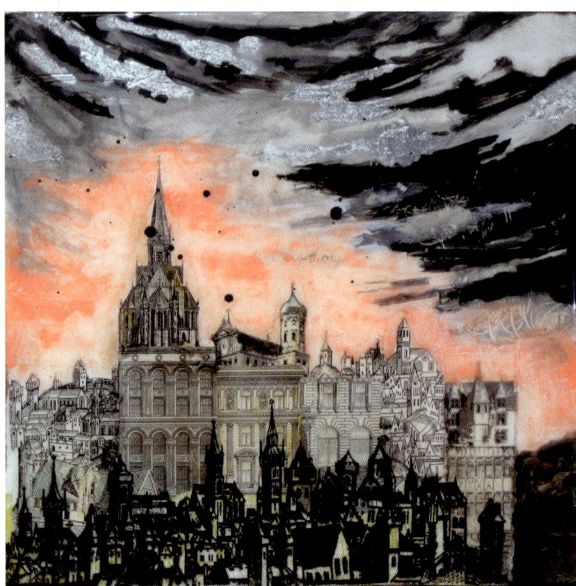

And here you find me in the shades of twilight · *gelatine silverprint & mixed media*

Scott Holloway · USA

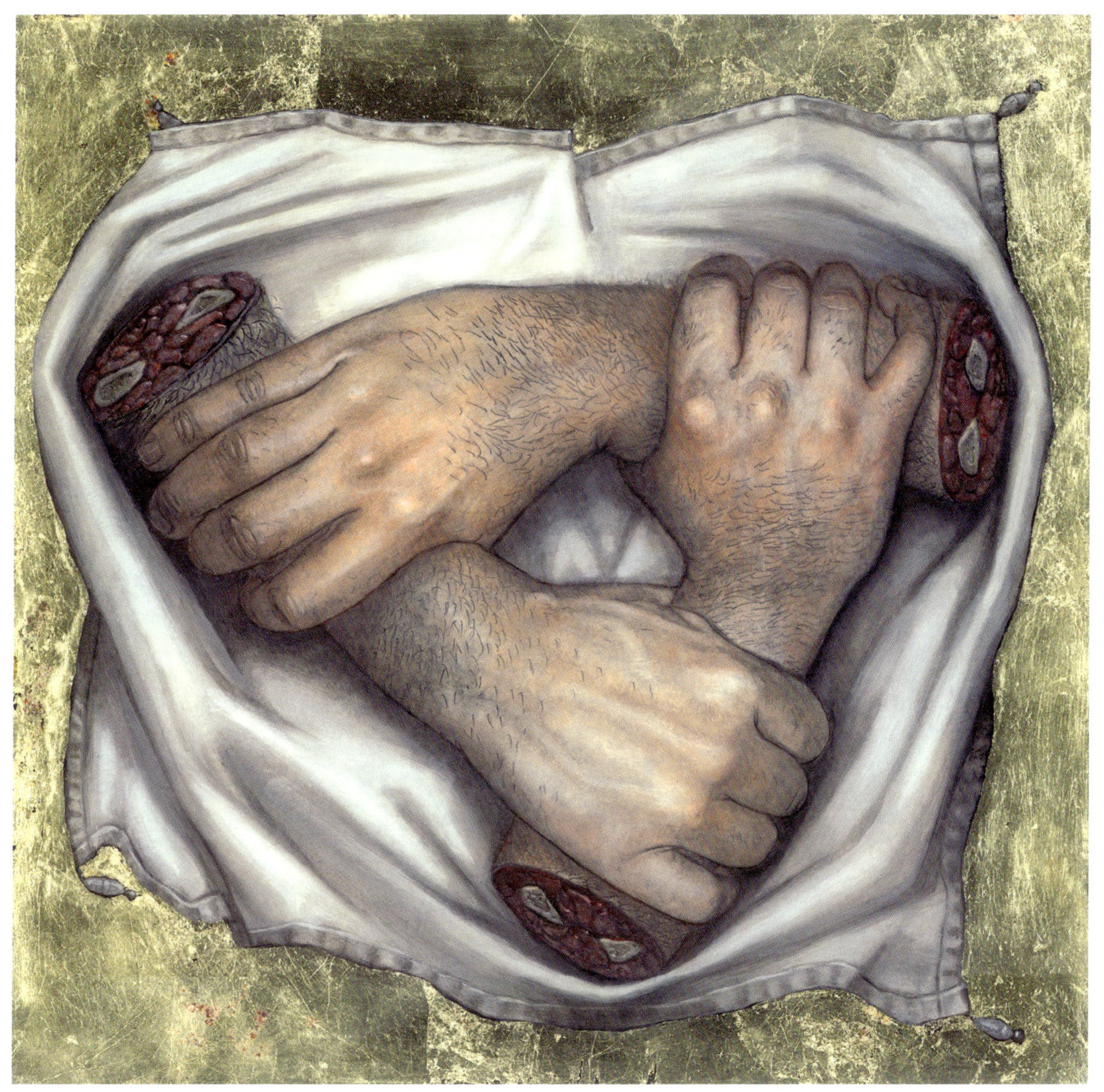

Three Wise Men · *oil, ink & leaf on panel*

Tommas Jørgensen · Denmark

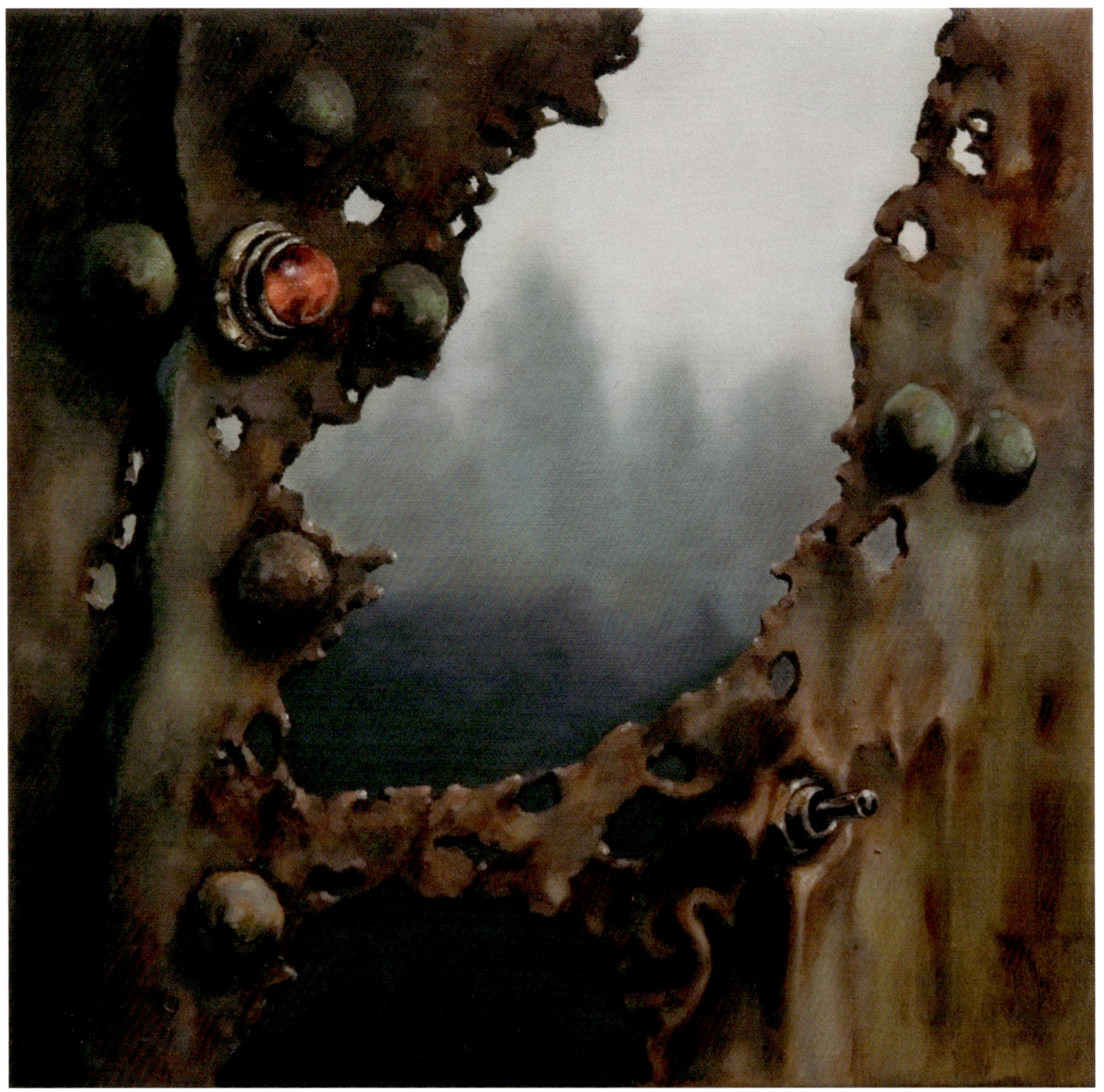

Dementia 1 · *oil on canvas*

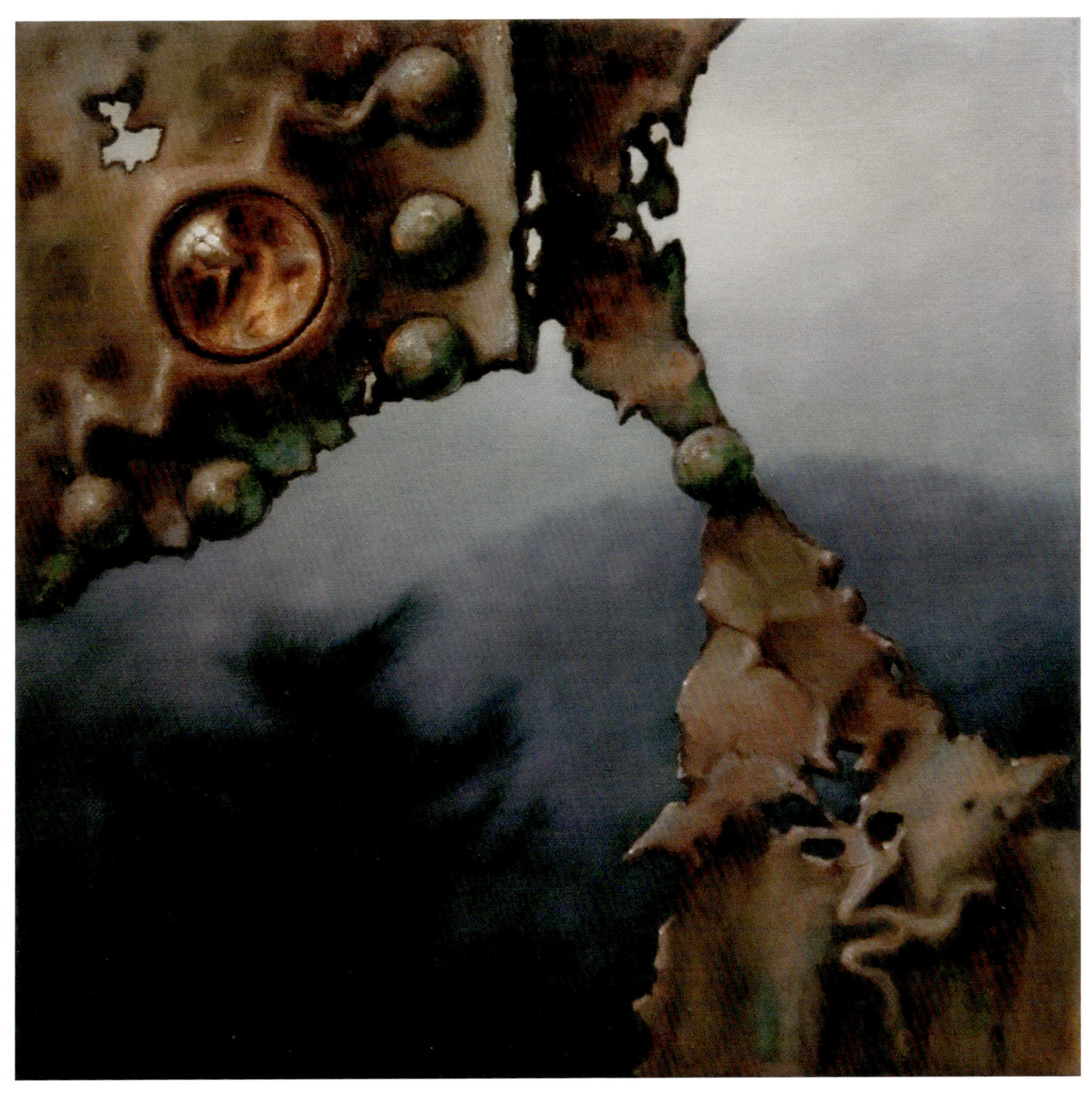

Dementia 2 · *oil on canvas*

Lisa Mei Ling Fong · USA

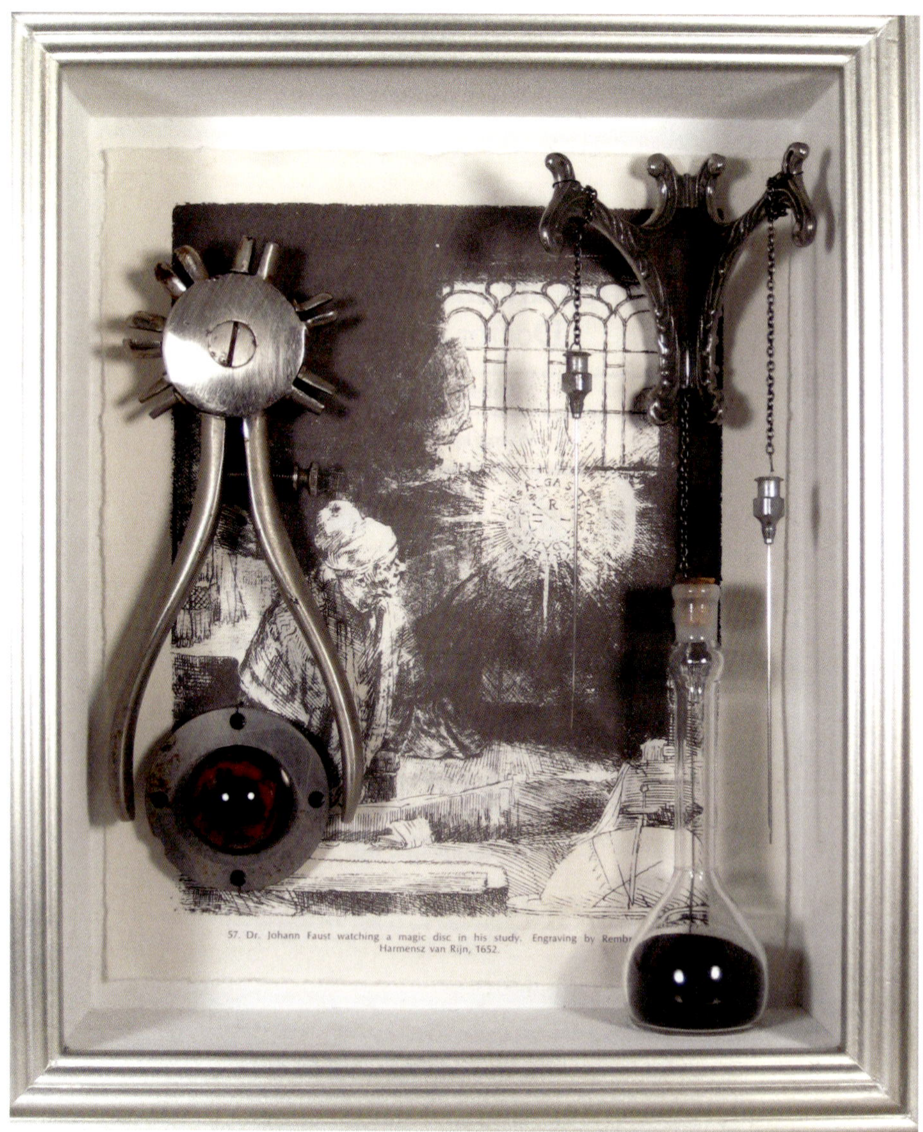

Faust *"introversion Box" · mixed media*

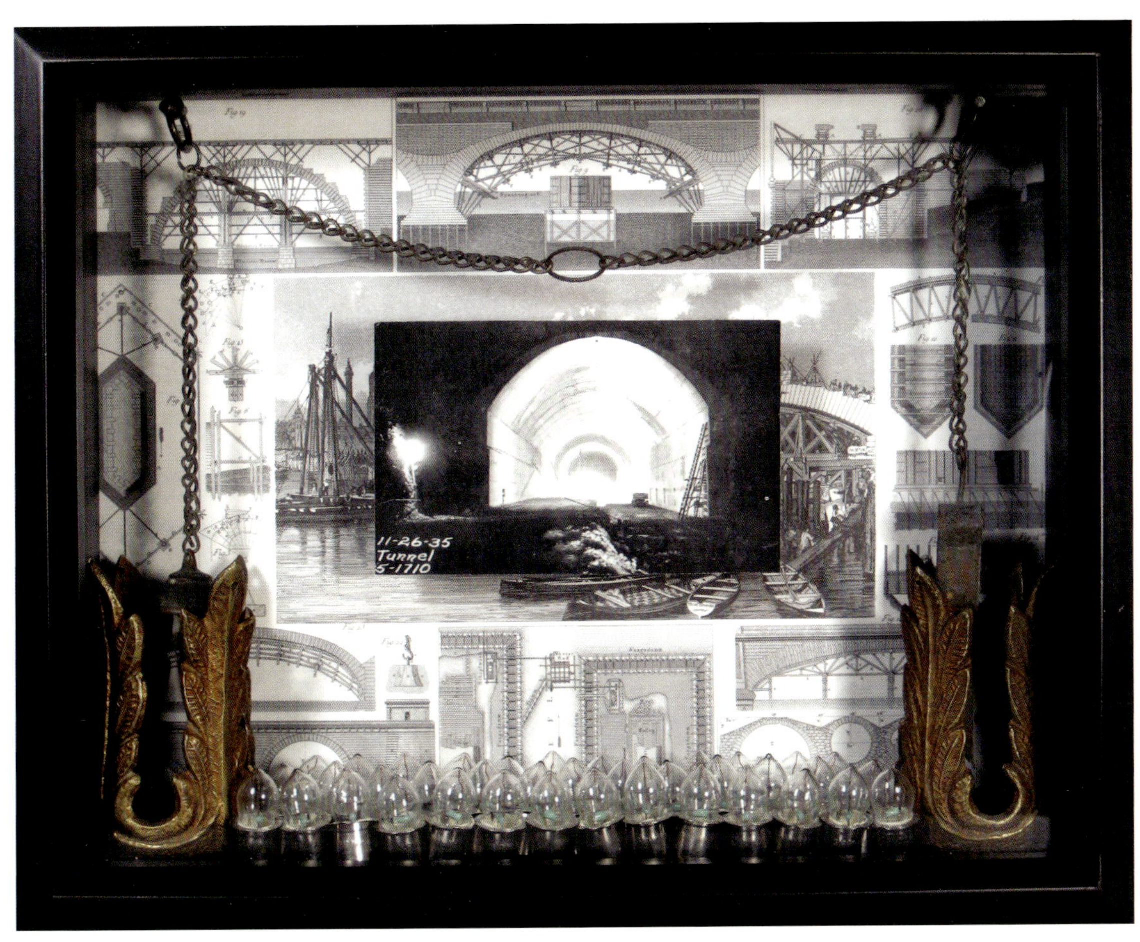

Light *"introversion Box" · mixed media*

Lukáš Kándl · Czech Rep.

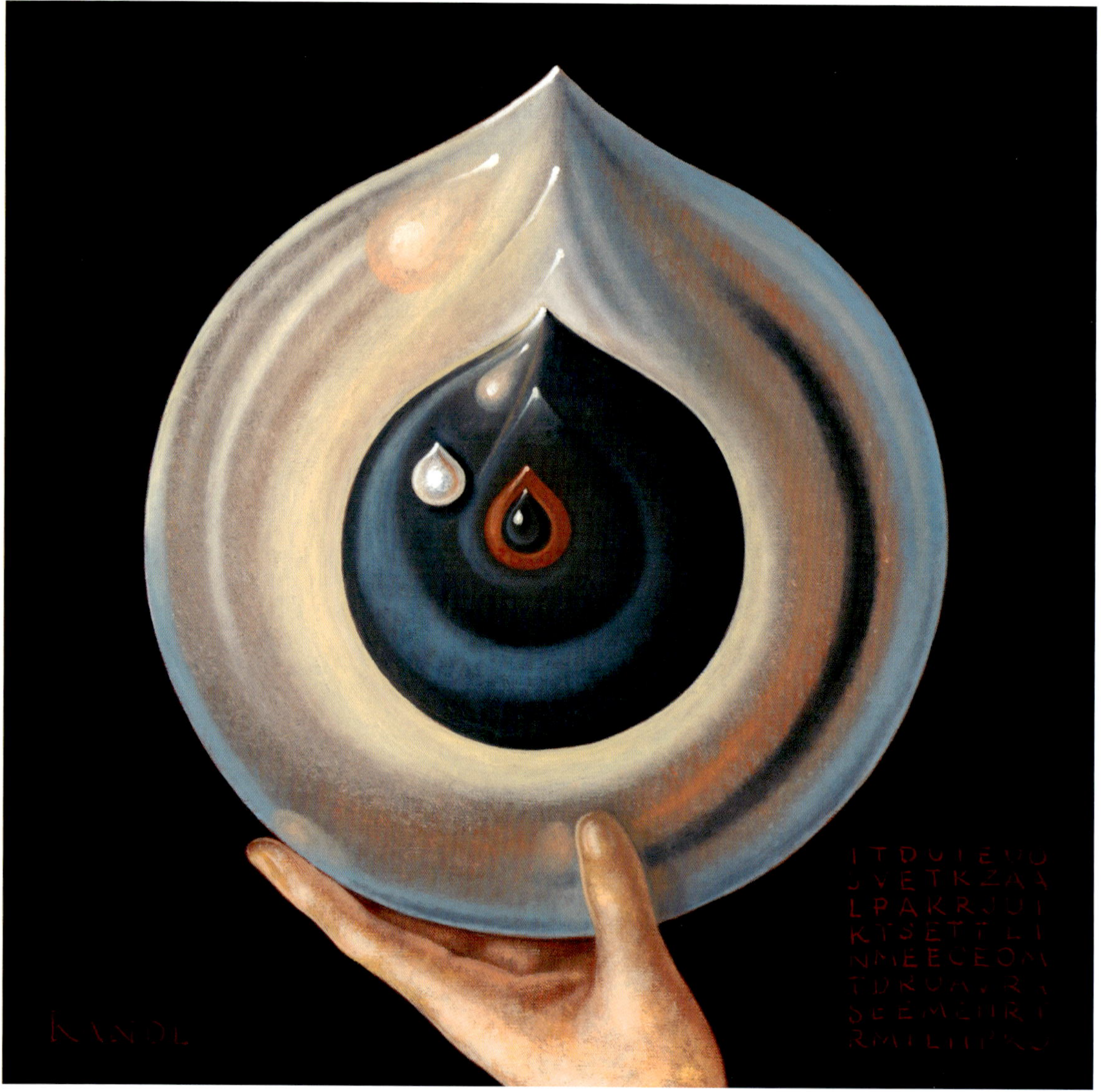

I bring you a drop · *oil on canvas*

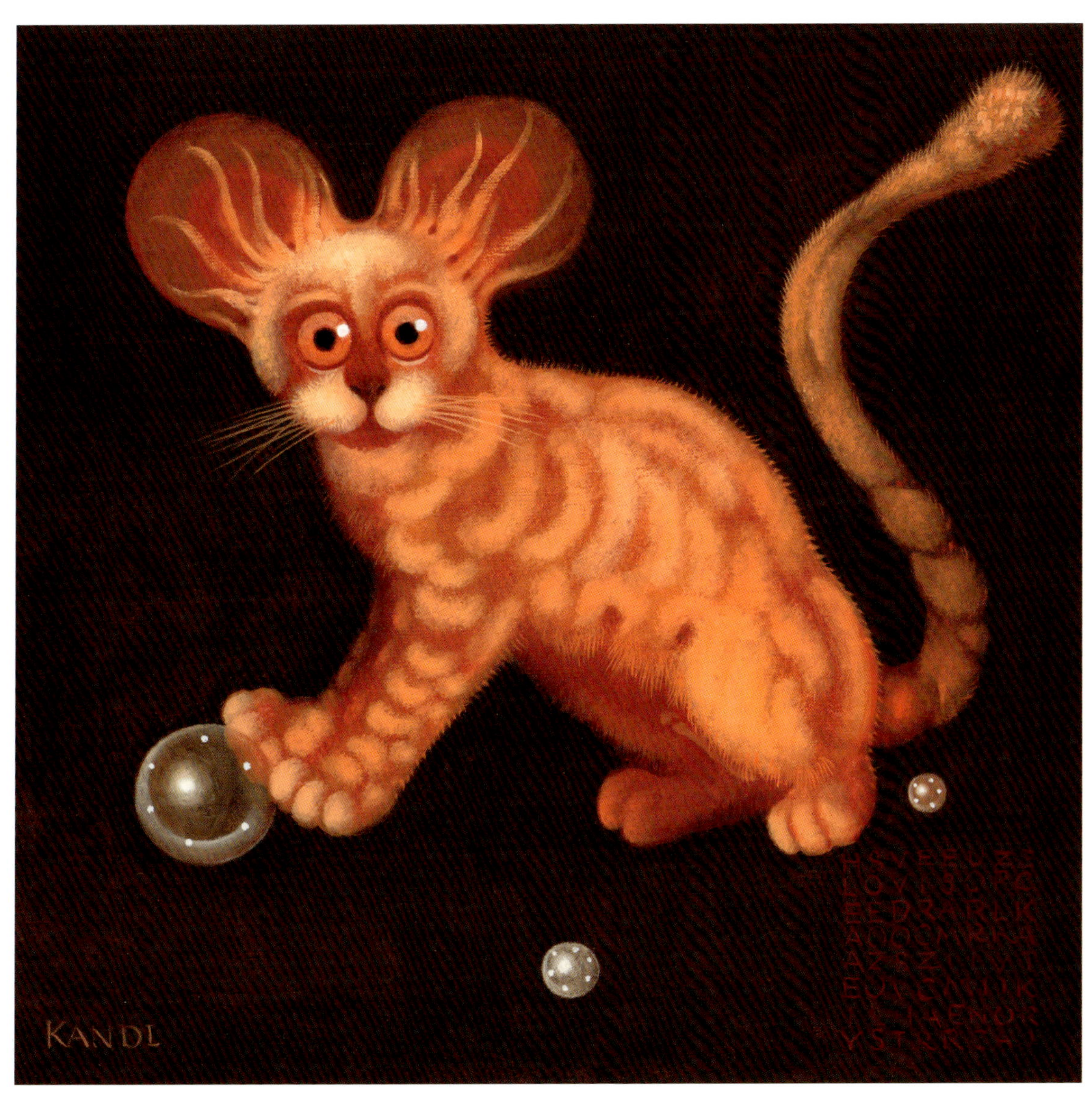

Strange little animal · *oil on canvas*

Steven Kenny · USA

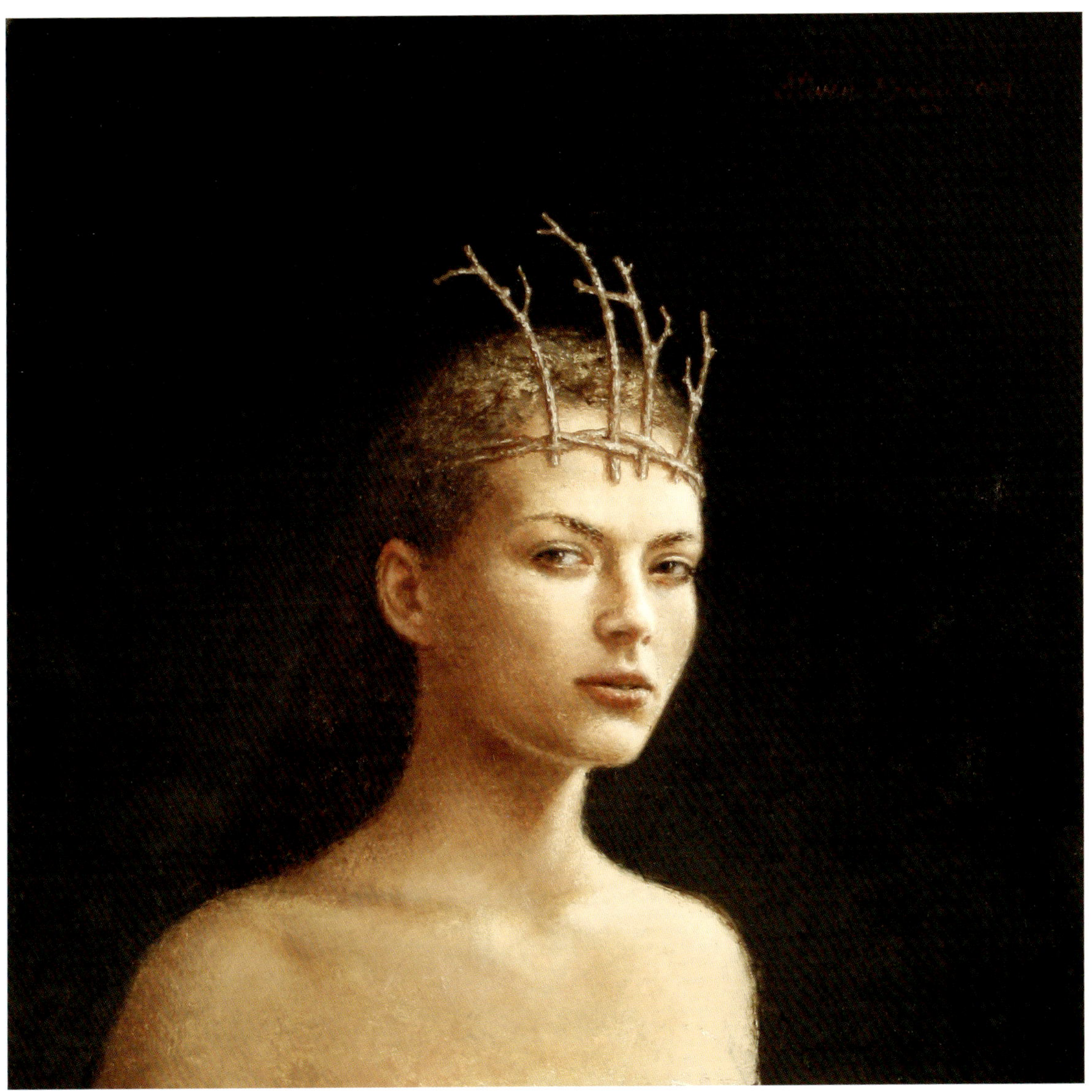

The Twig Tiara · *oil on panel*

Richard Kirk · England

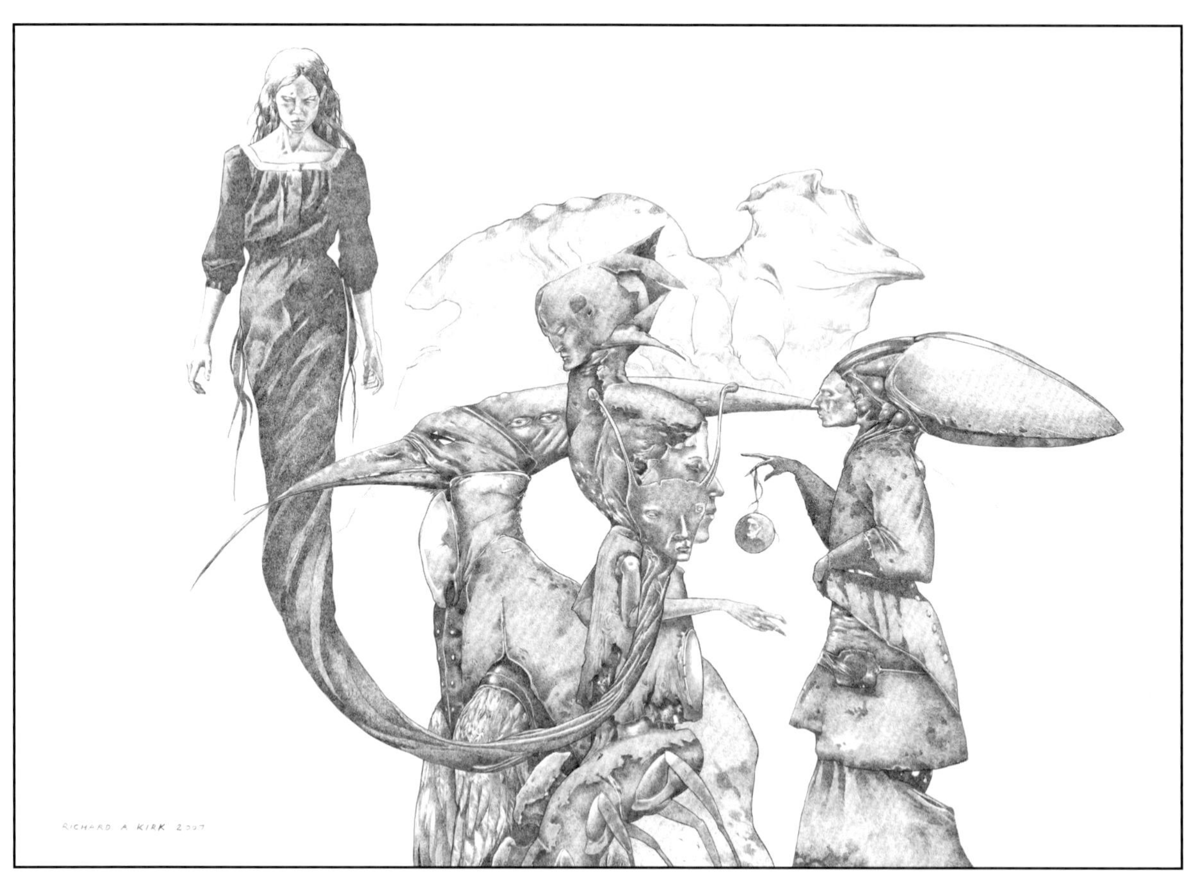

Hellbender · *ink on paper*

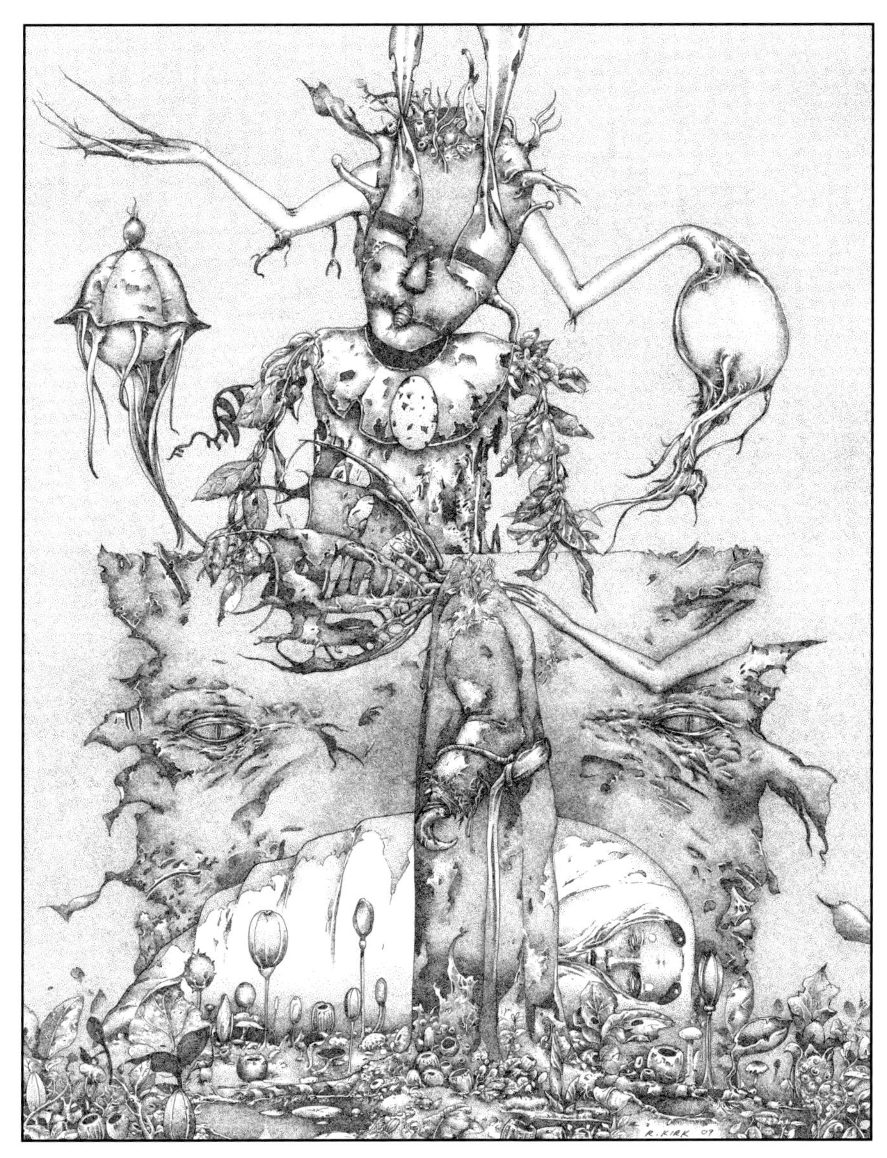

Awakening · *ink on paper*

Dirk Larsen · England

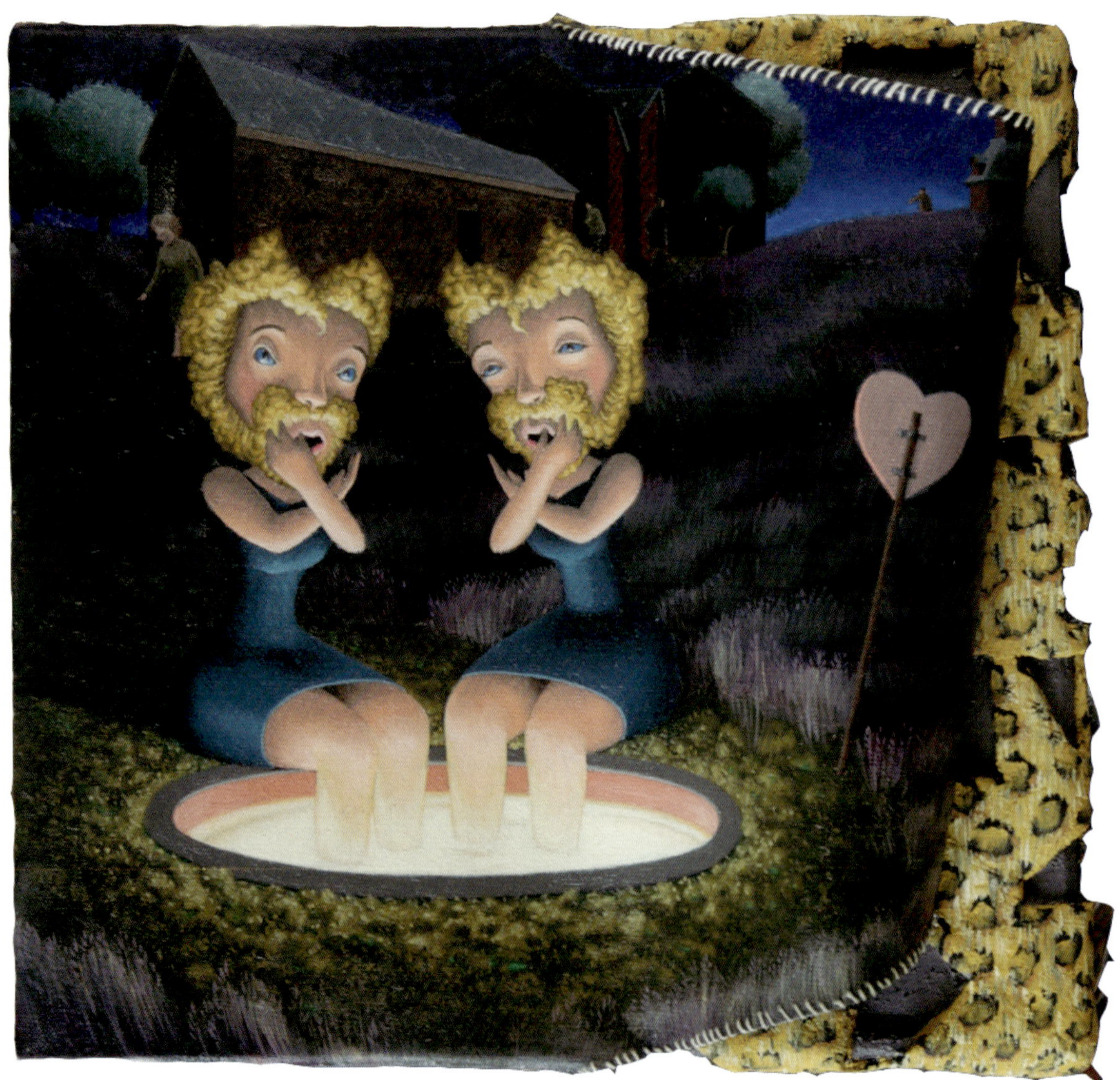

The Twincesses of Beard · *oil on various material*

Edith Lebeau · Canada

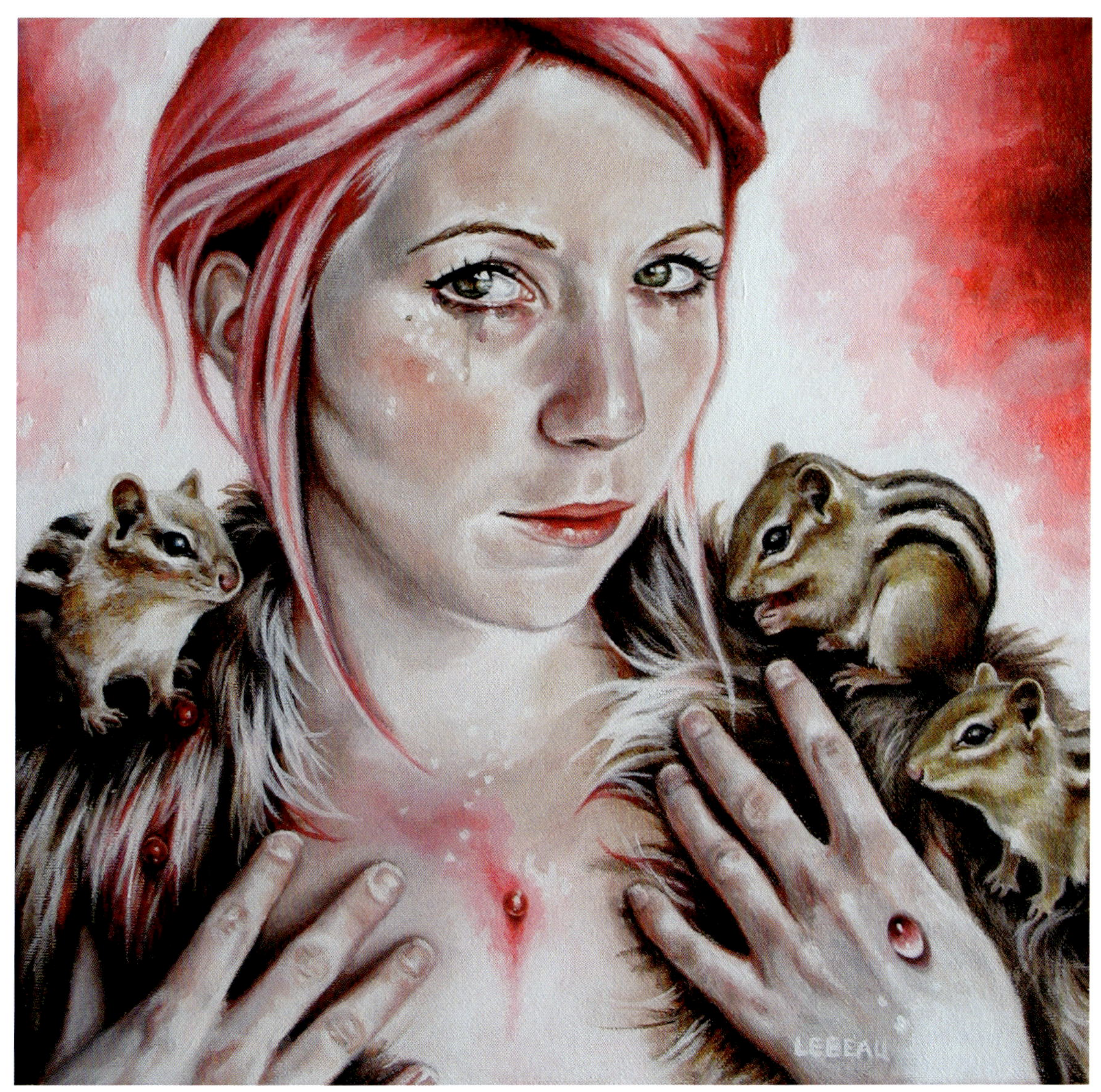

Berries girl · *acrylic on canvas*

Gary Lippencott · USA

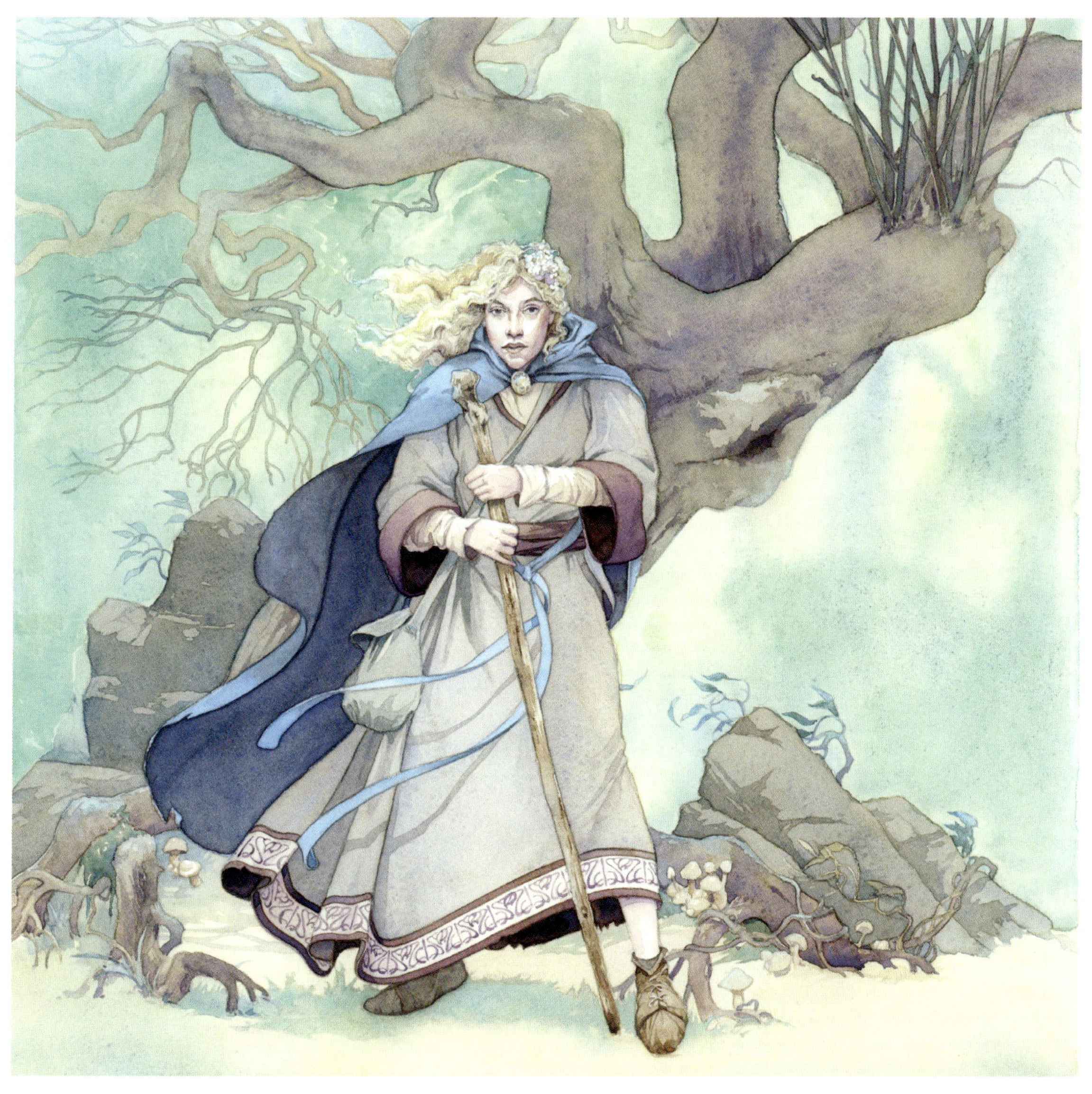

Apprentice · *watercolour*

Micha Lobi · Sibiria

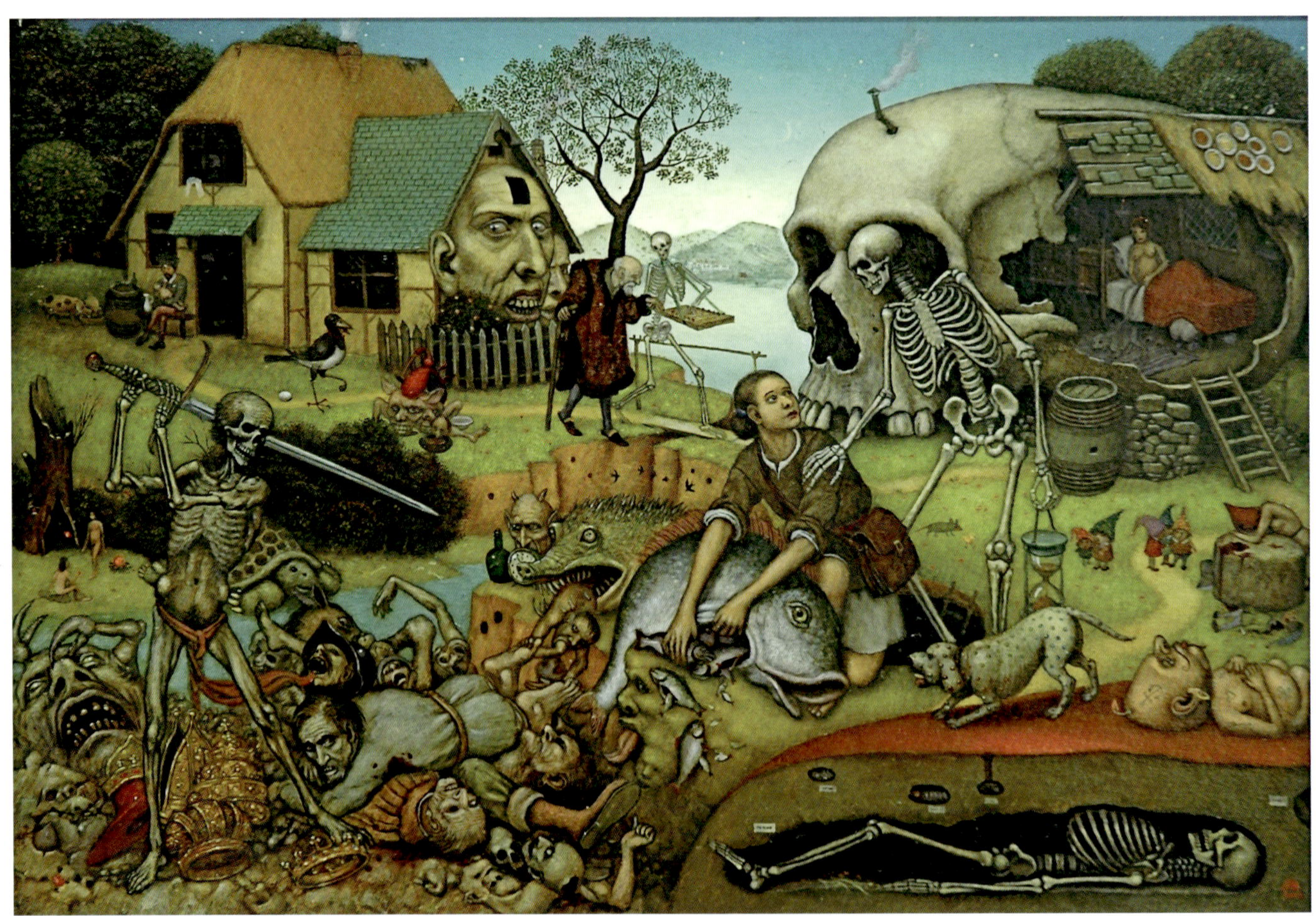

Between the houses · *oil & tempera on panel*

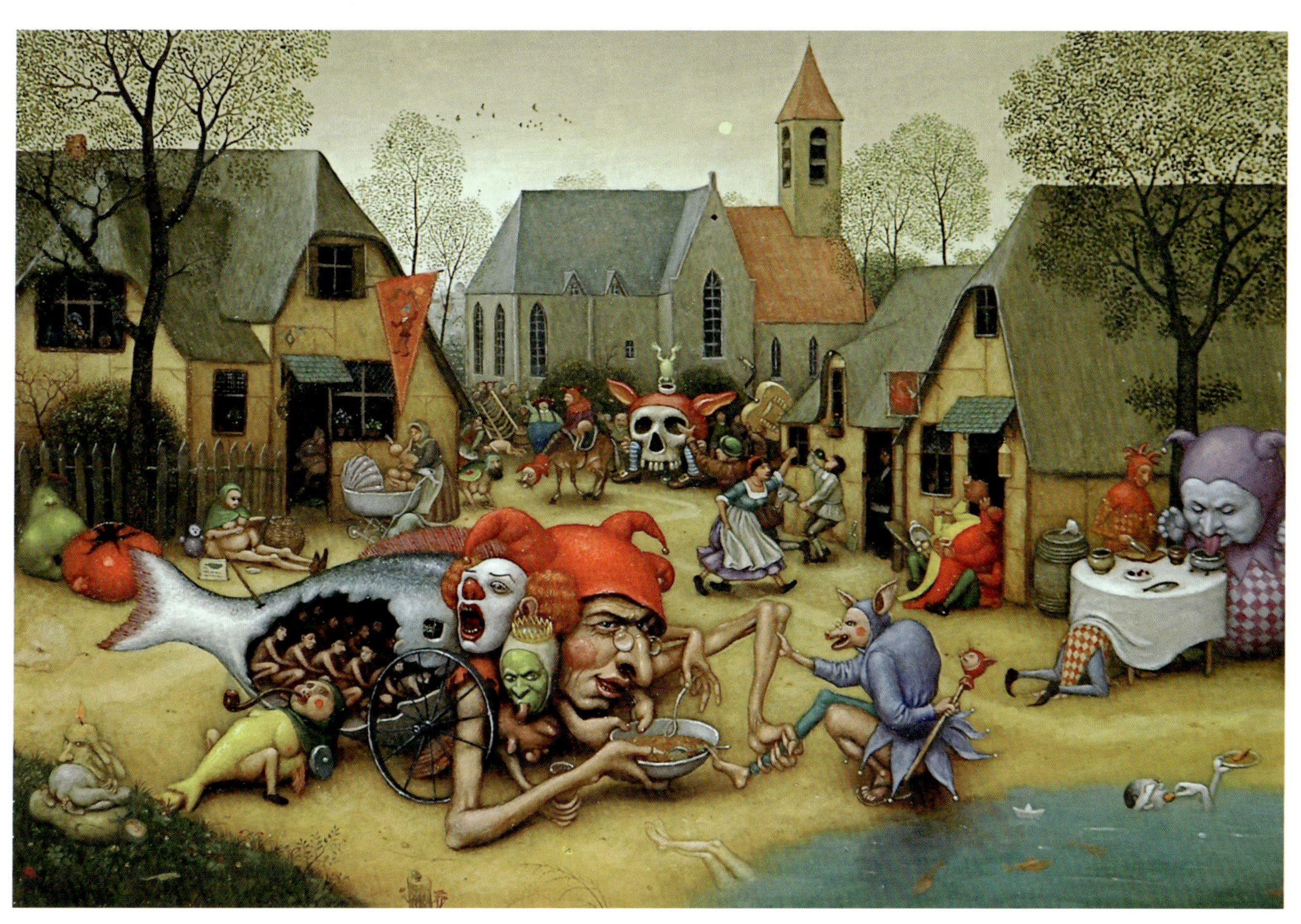

The Day of The Fish · *oil & tempera on panel*

Ludmila · Portugal

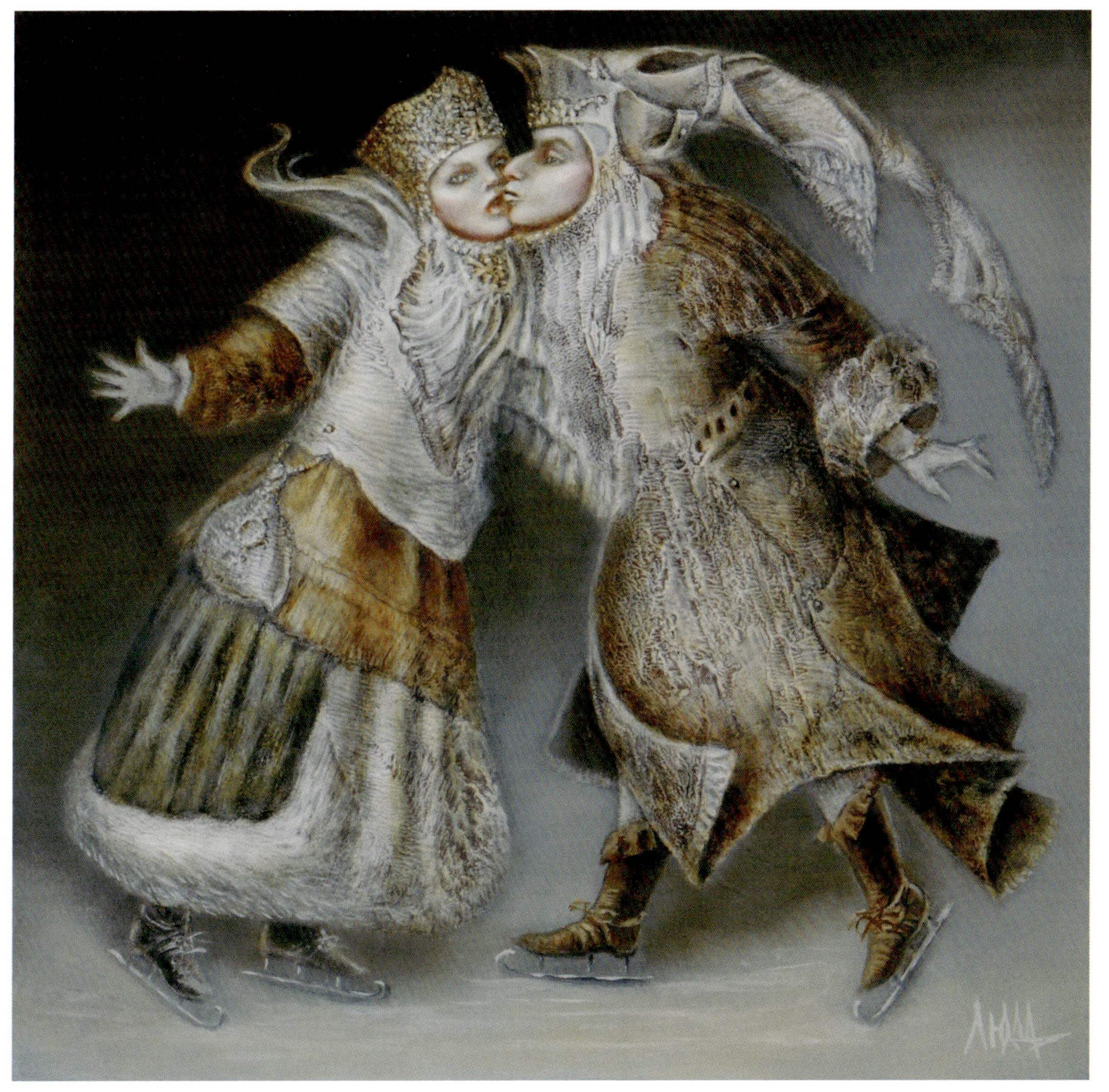

Accidental Kiss · *oil on panel*

Ver Mar · USA

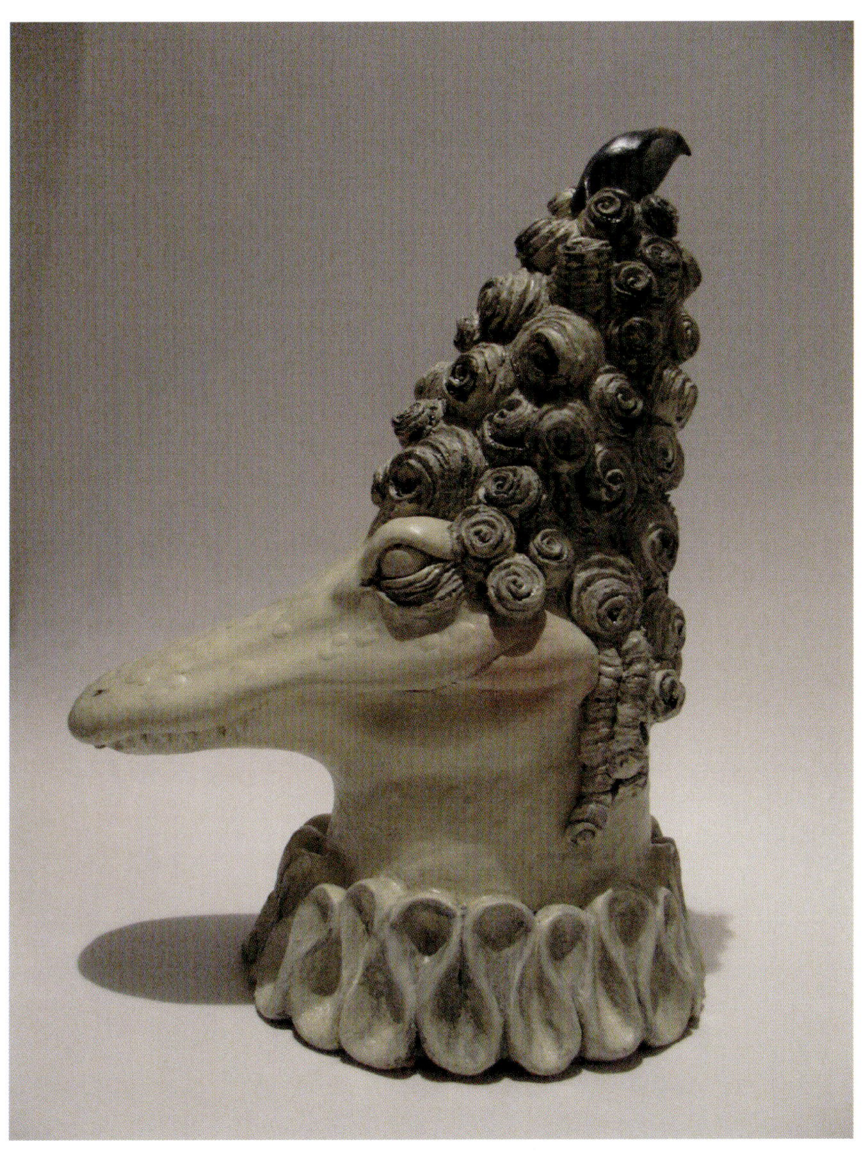

Keeping up Appearances · *clay & acrylic sculpture*

Bethany Marchman · USA

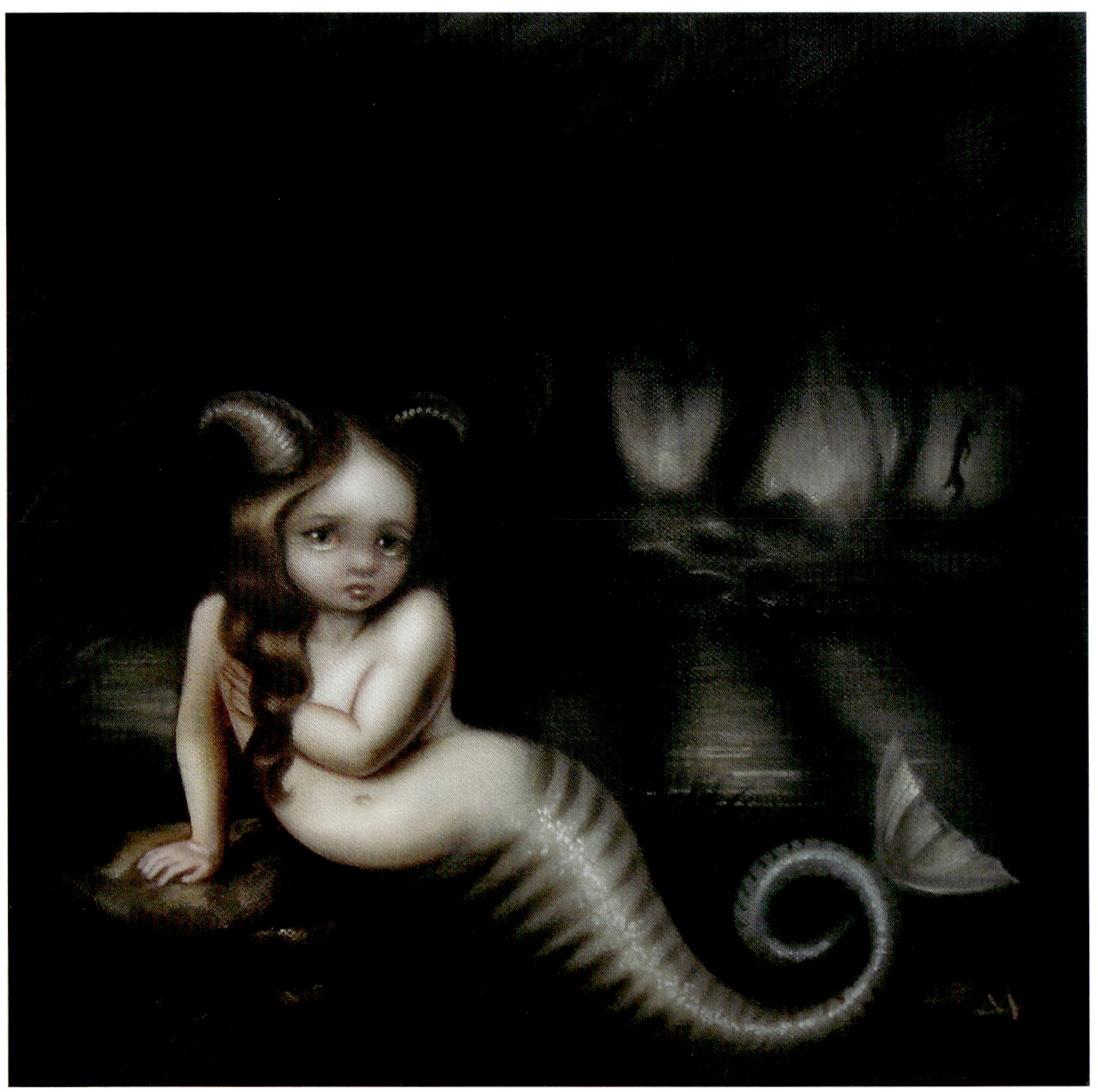

Capricorn · *oil on canvas*

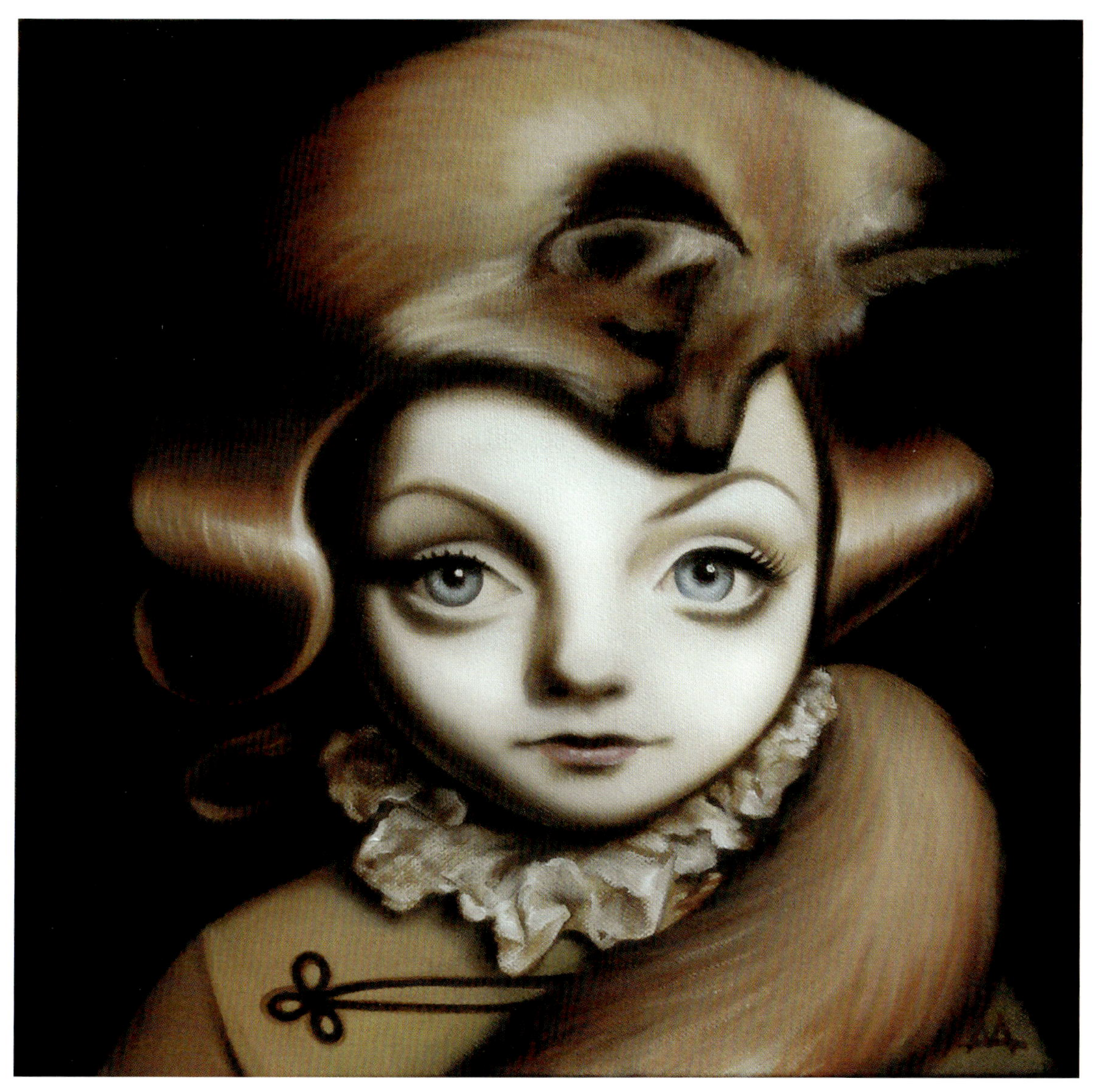

Fox Hunt · *oil on canvas*

William McDermitt · England

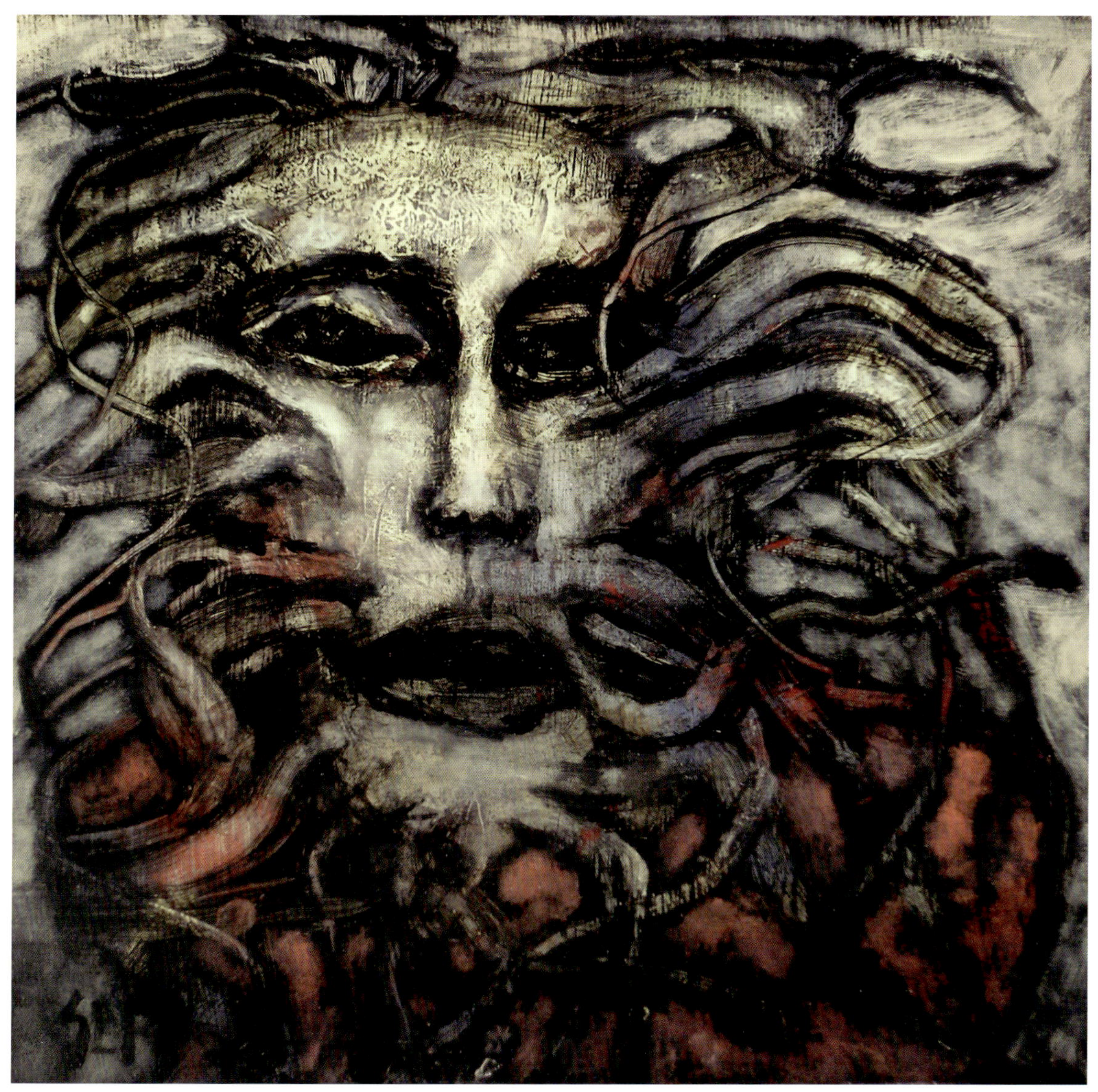

Love is Unravelling · *oil on panel*

Ansgar Noeth · Germany

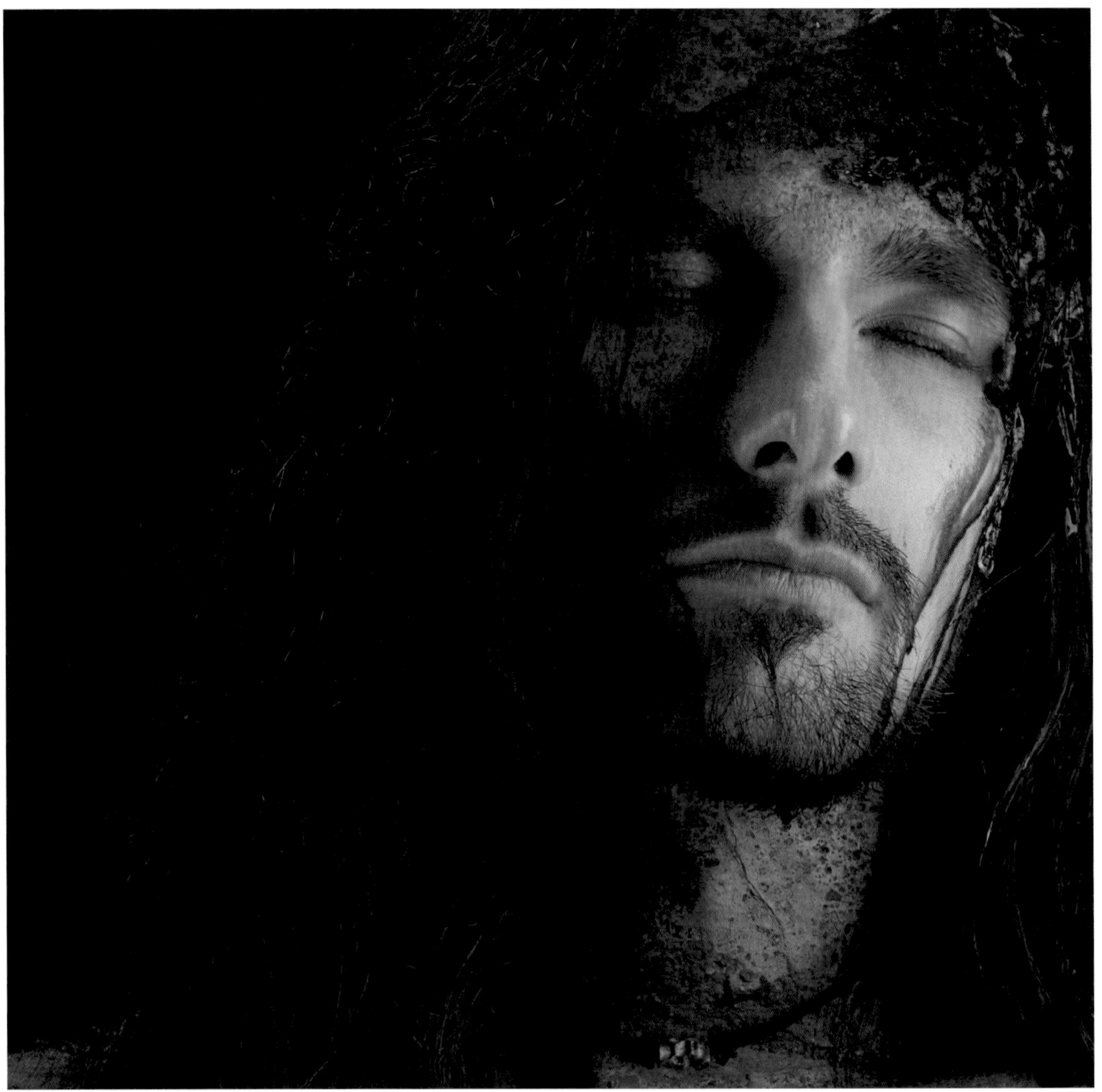

Hurt 1 · *photographic print on glass*

Voytek Nowakowski · Canada

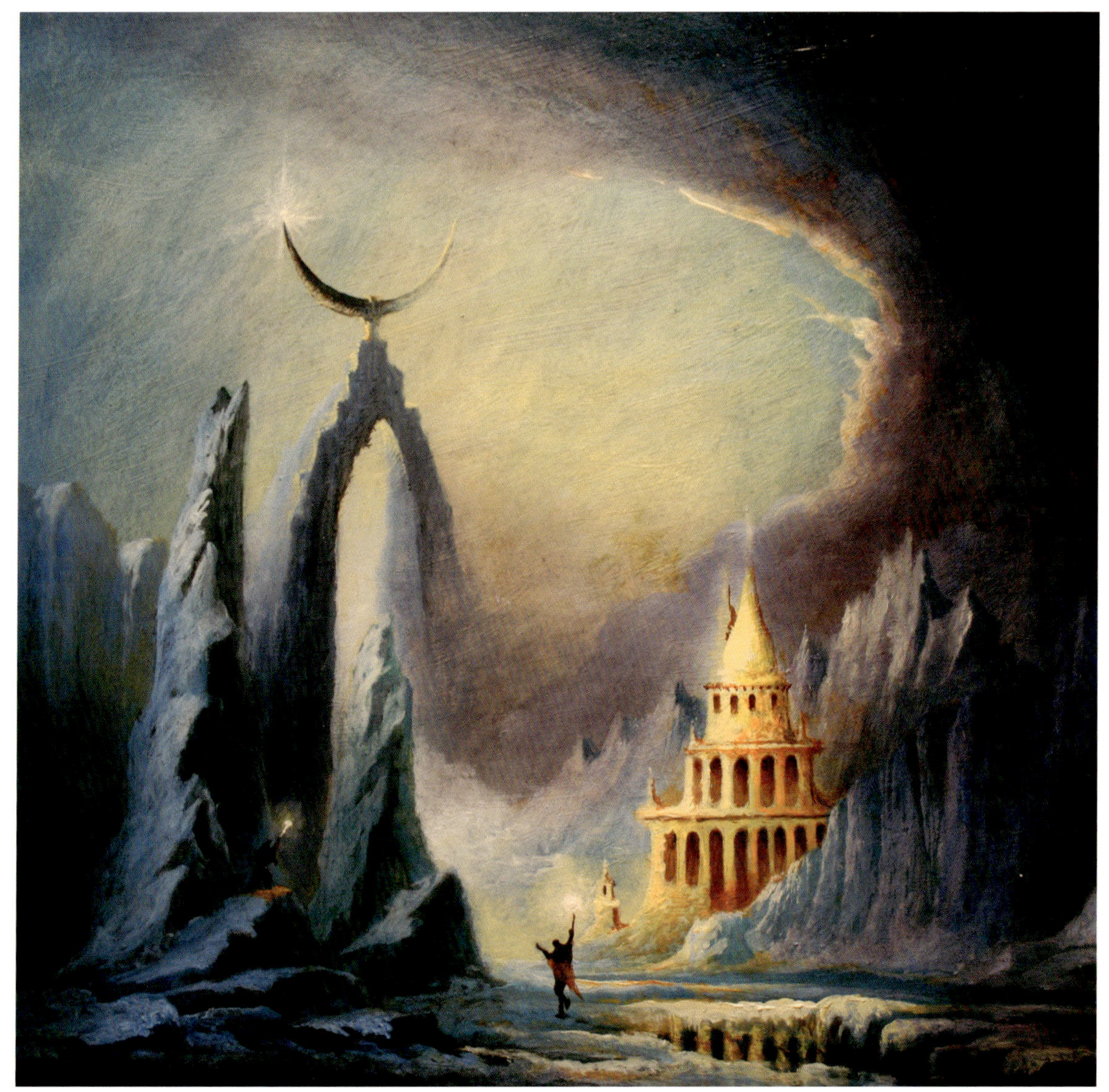

Winter Sanctuary · *oil on panel*

Peter van Oostzanen · Netherlands

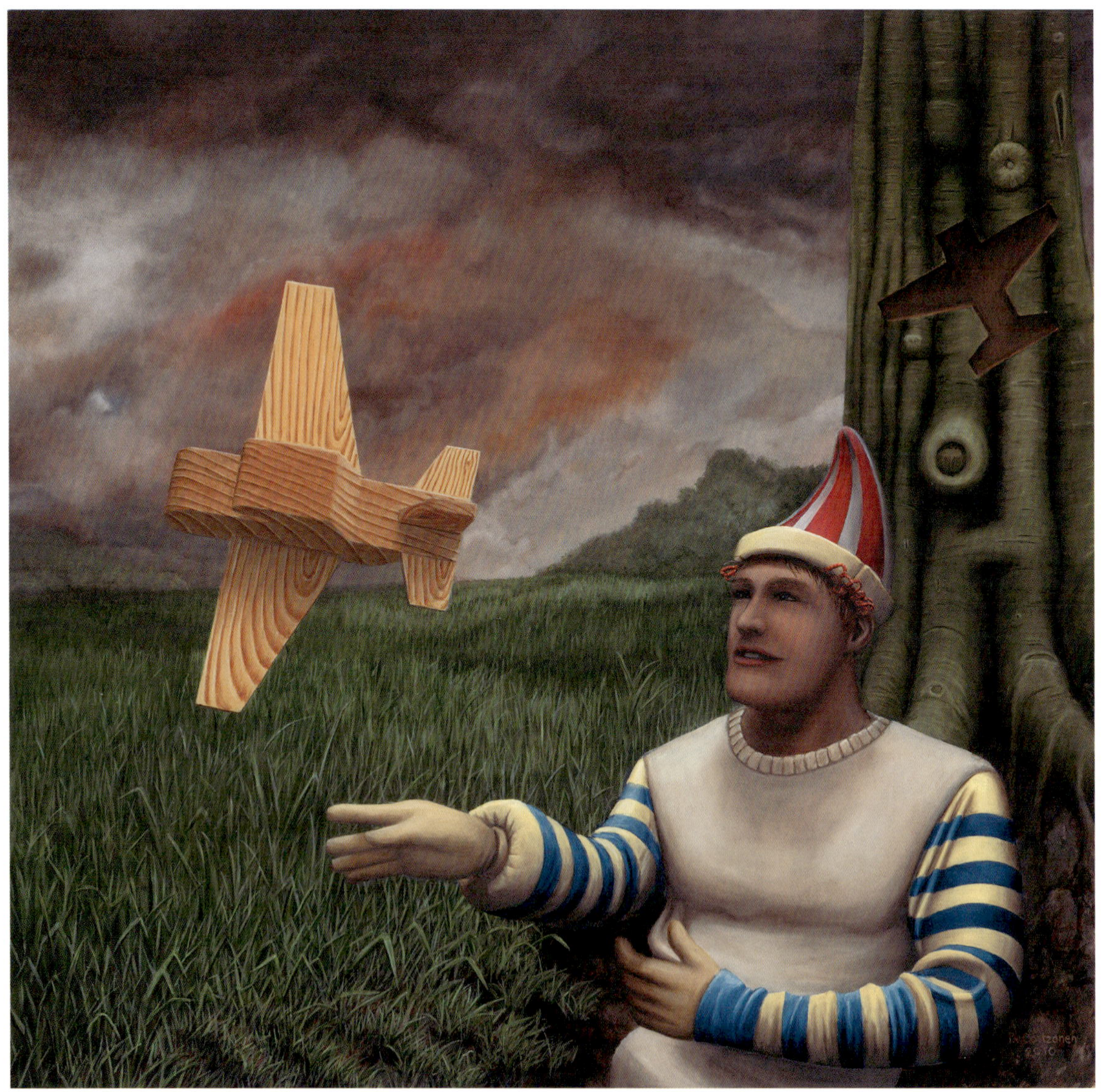

The Plane Baron · *oil on panel*

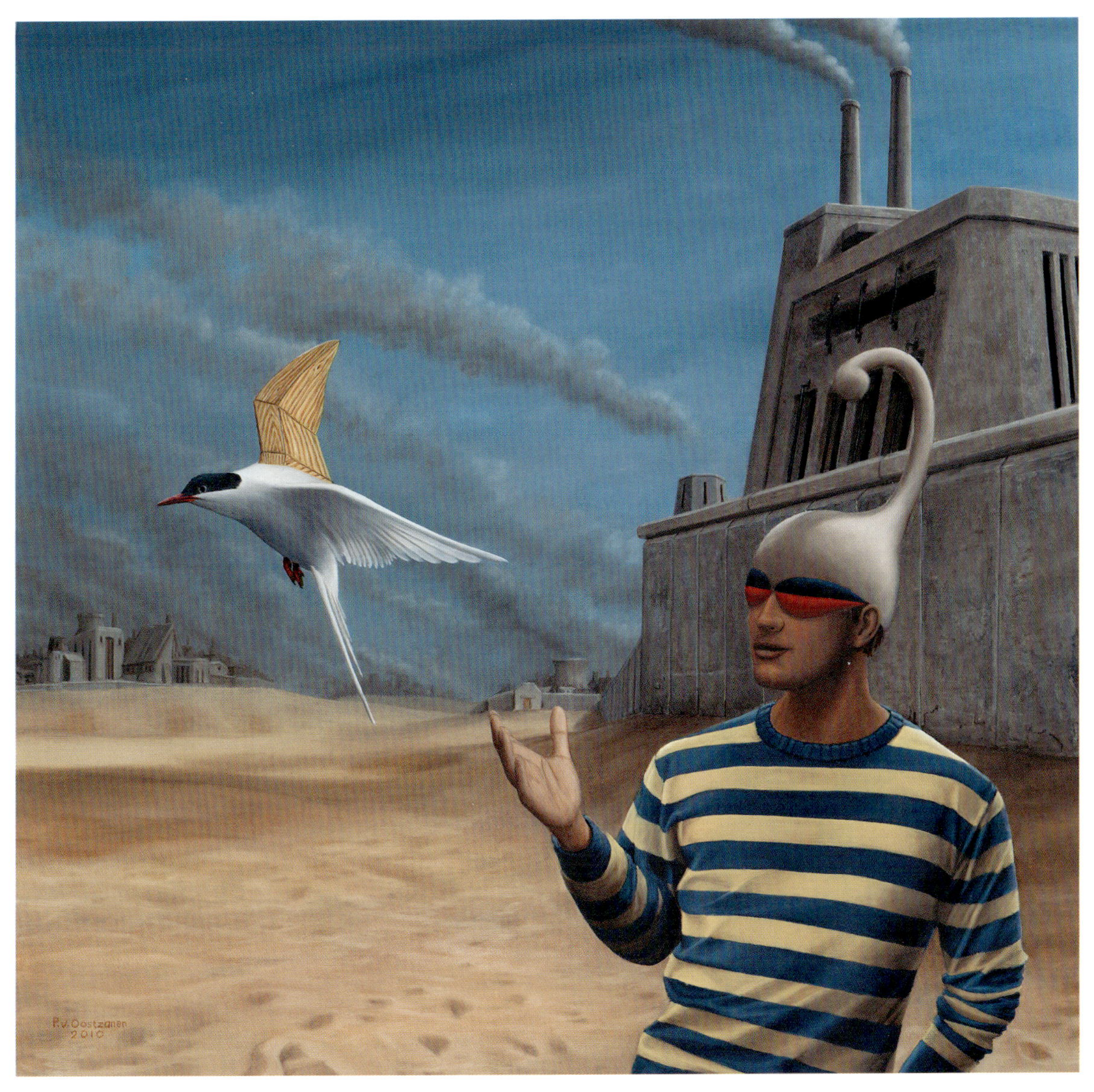

The Bird Repair · *oil on panel*

Jose Parra · Mexico

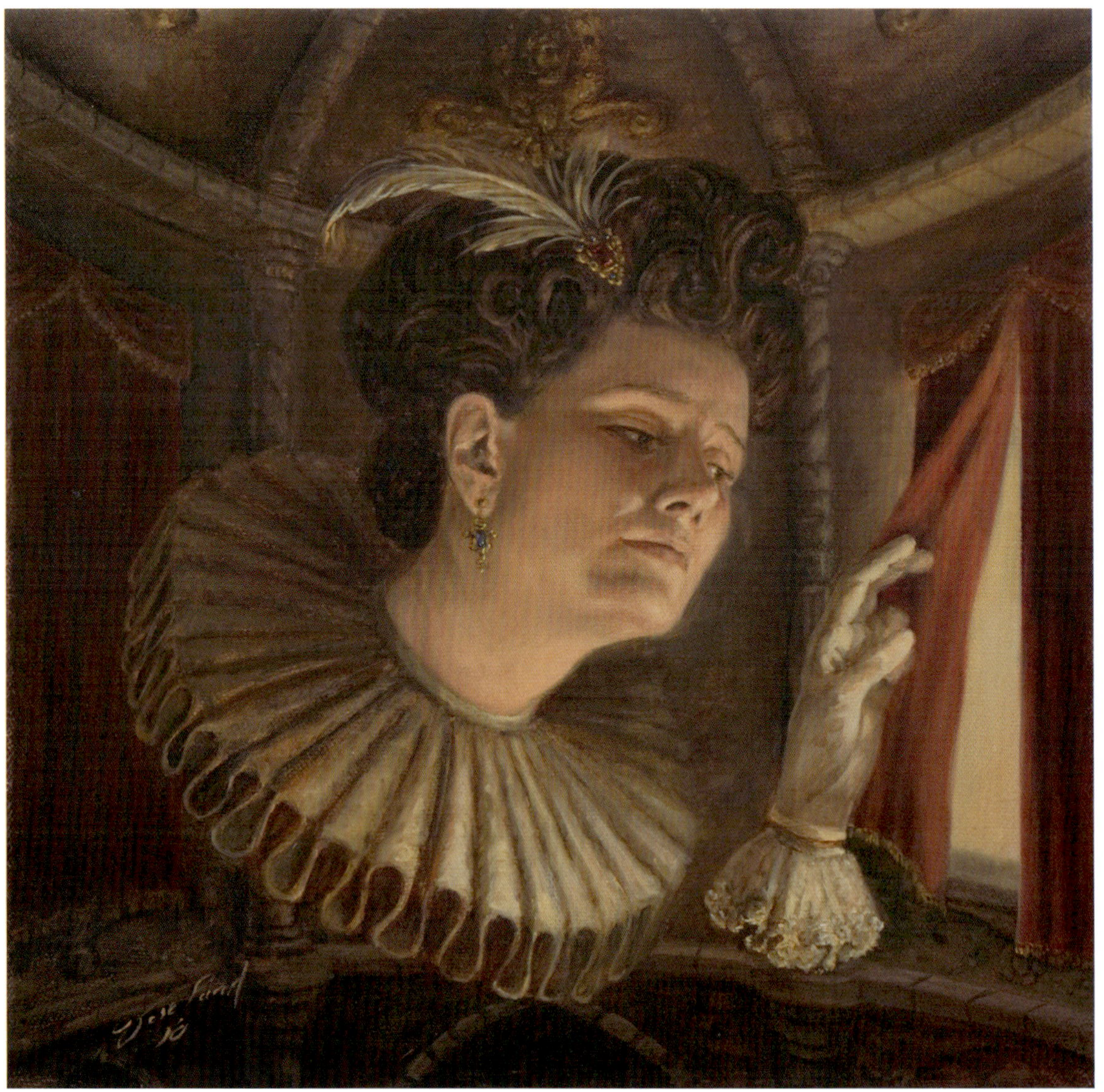

Someone's calling · *oil on canvas*

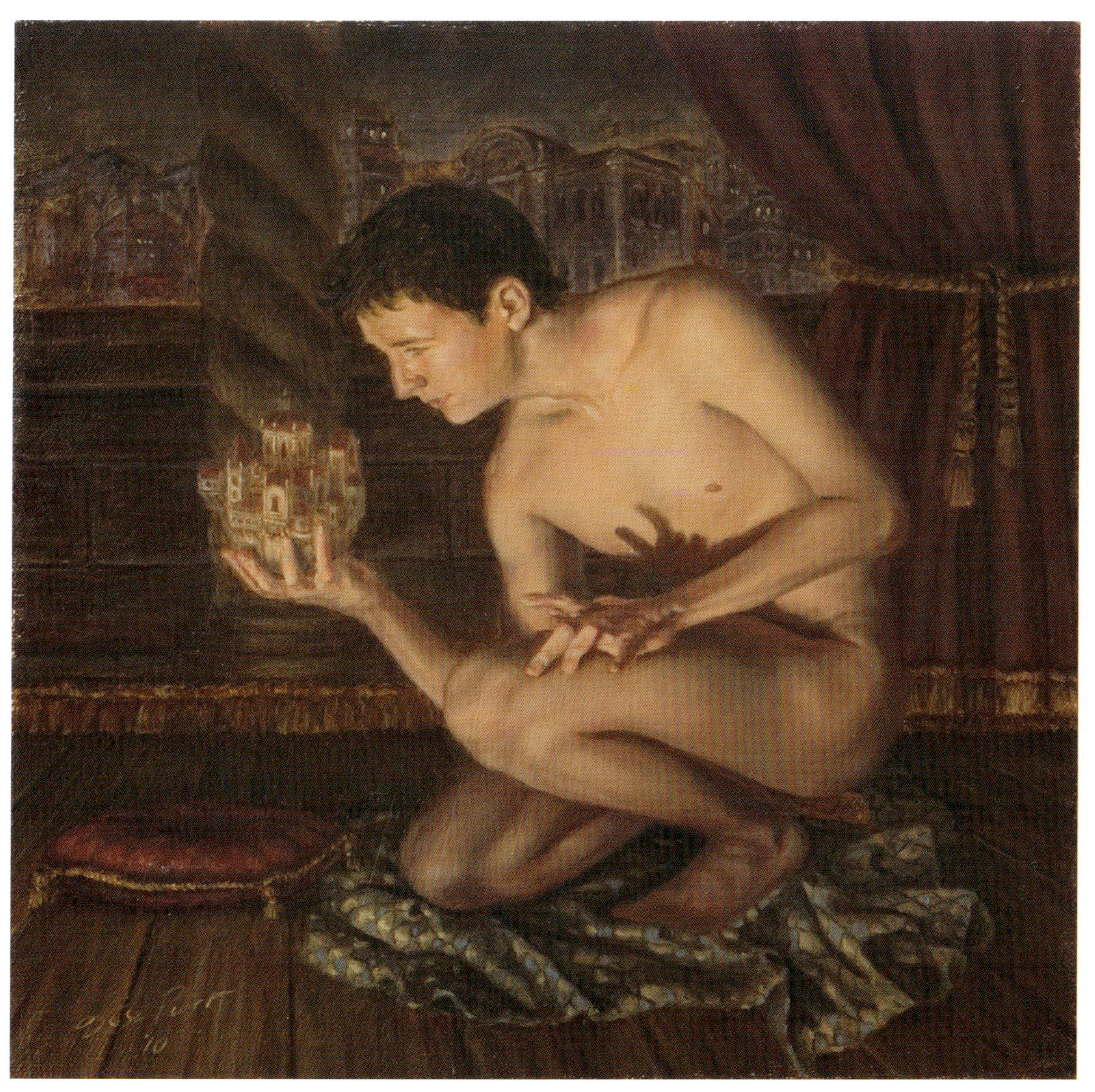

The caller · *oil on canvas*

Marcus Poston · USA

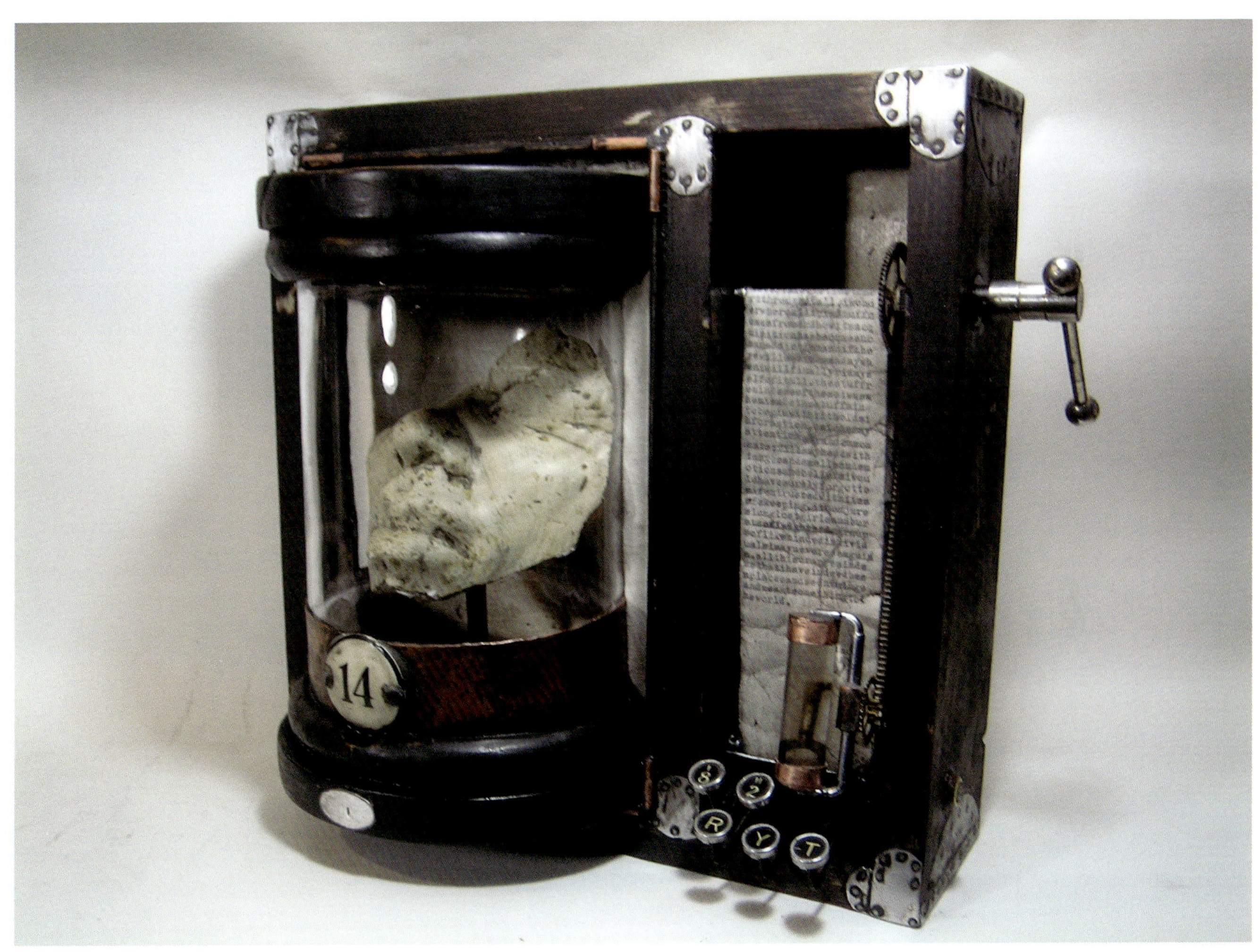

Valentine's Day · *mixed media sculpture*

Lee Harvey Roswell · USA

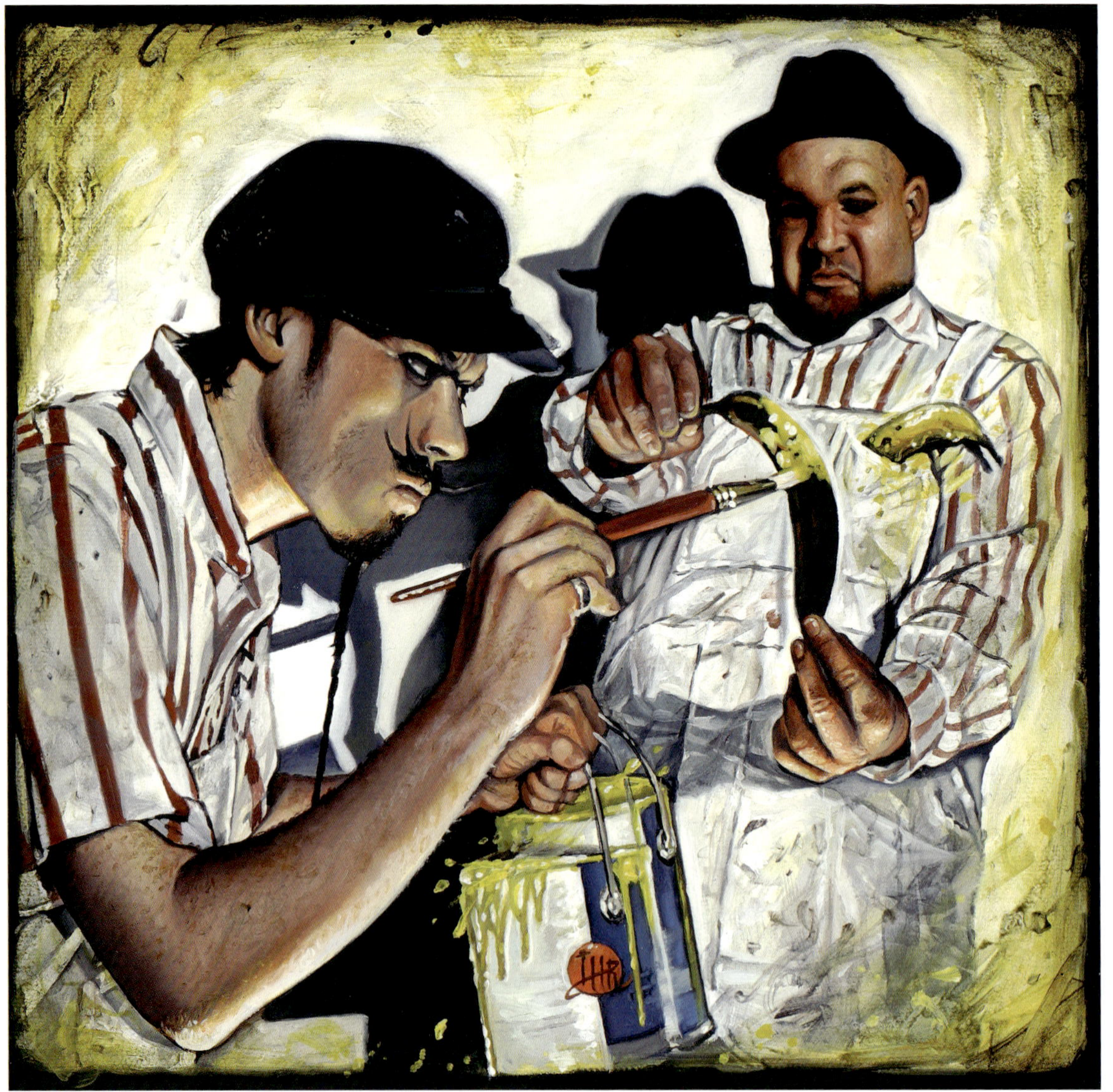

Touch-Ups for Resale · *oil on canvas*

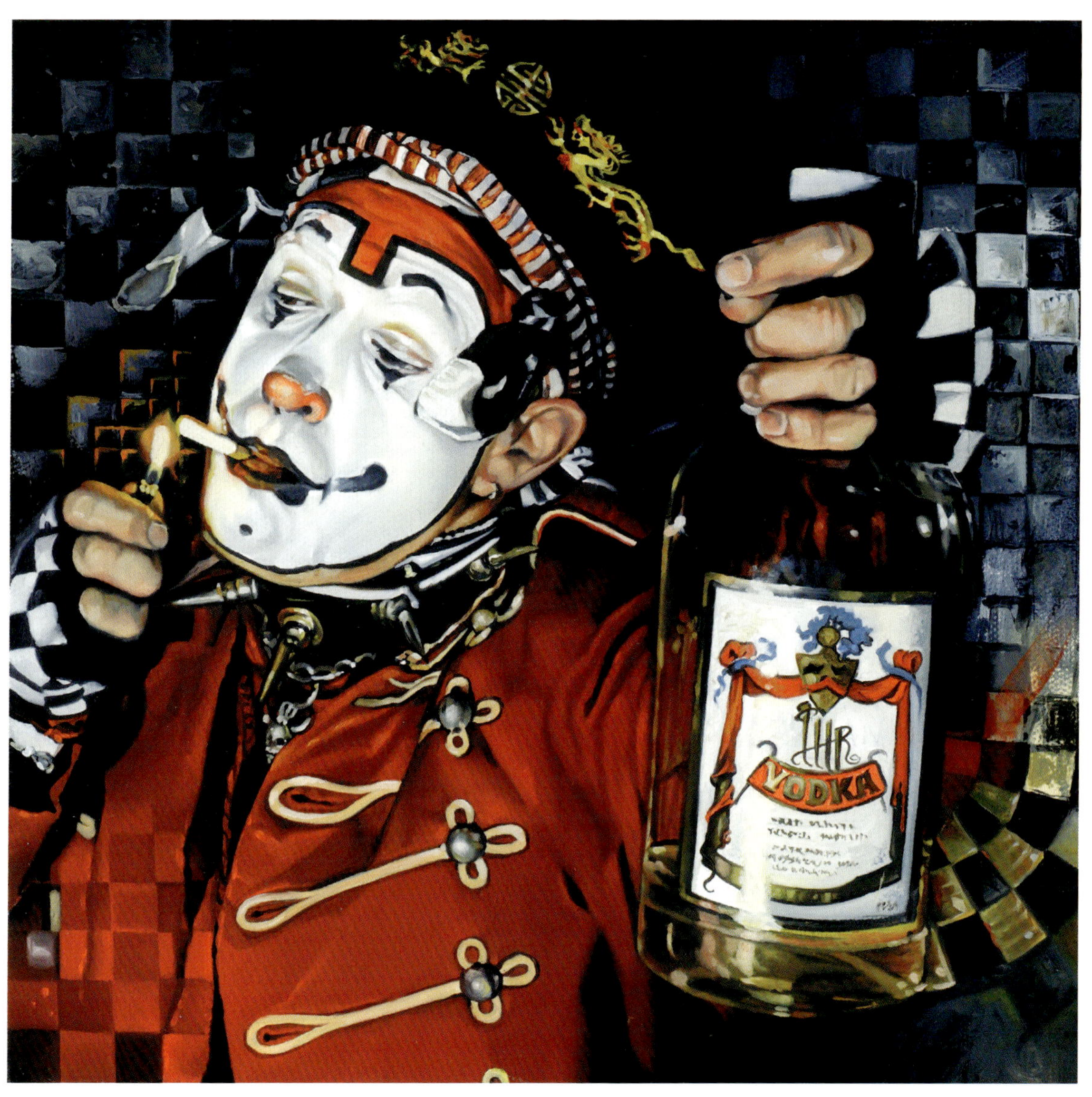

Checkered, Passed · *oil on canvas*

Tim Roosen · Belgium

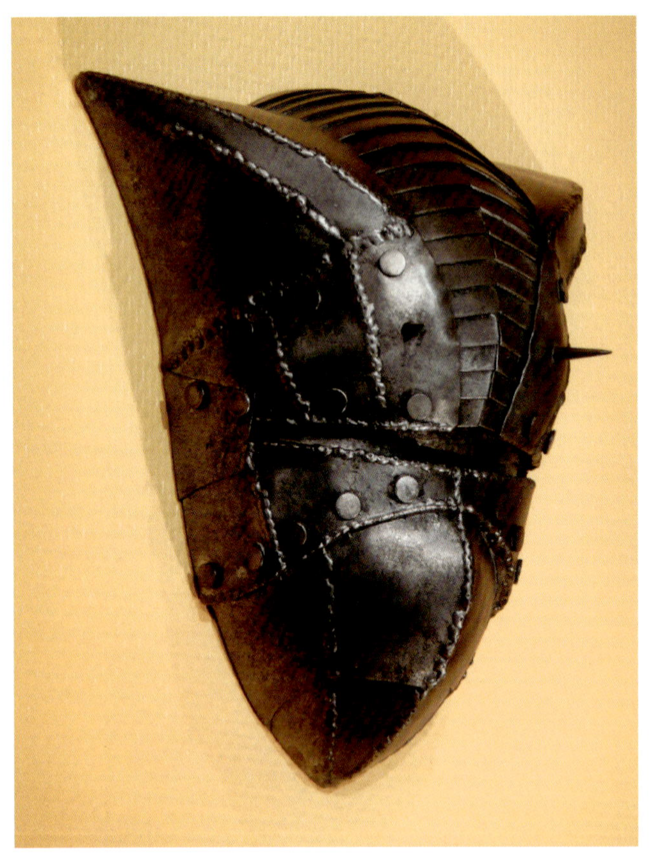

Captain · *mild steel, patinated*

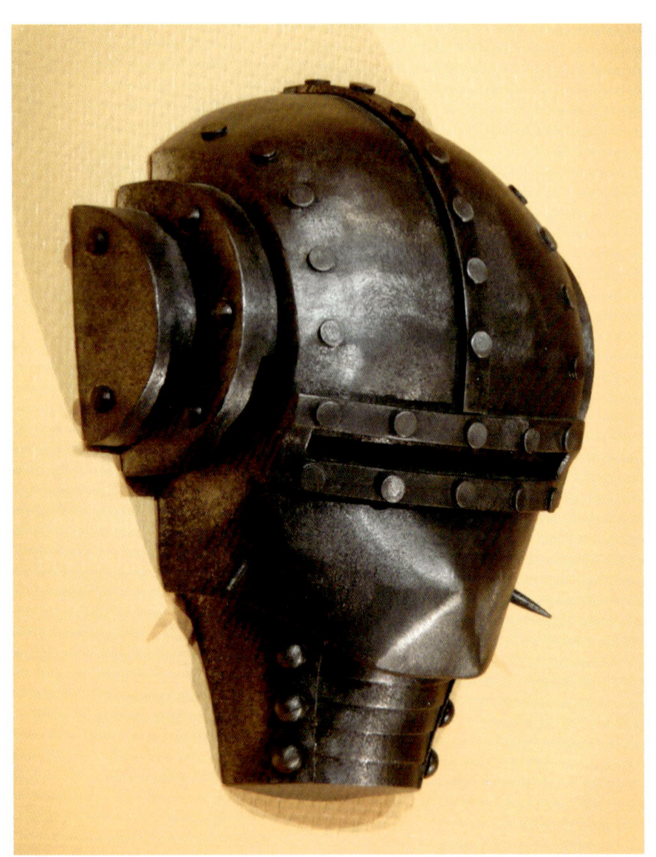

Major · *mild steel, patinated*

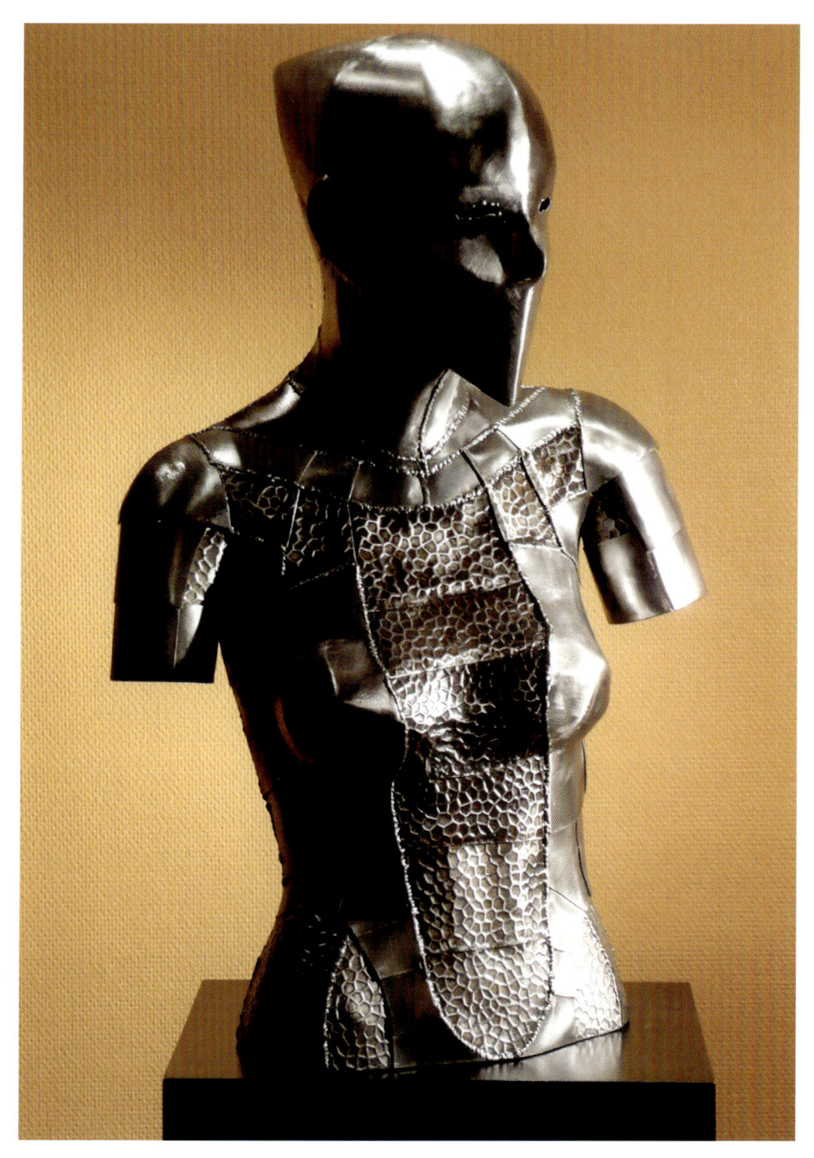

Rhiannon · *mild steel*

José Roosevelt · Brasil

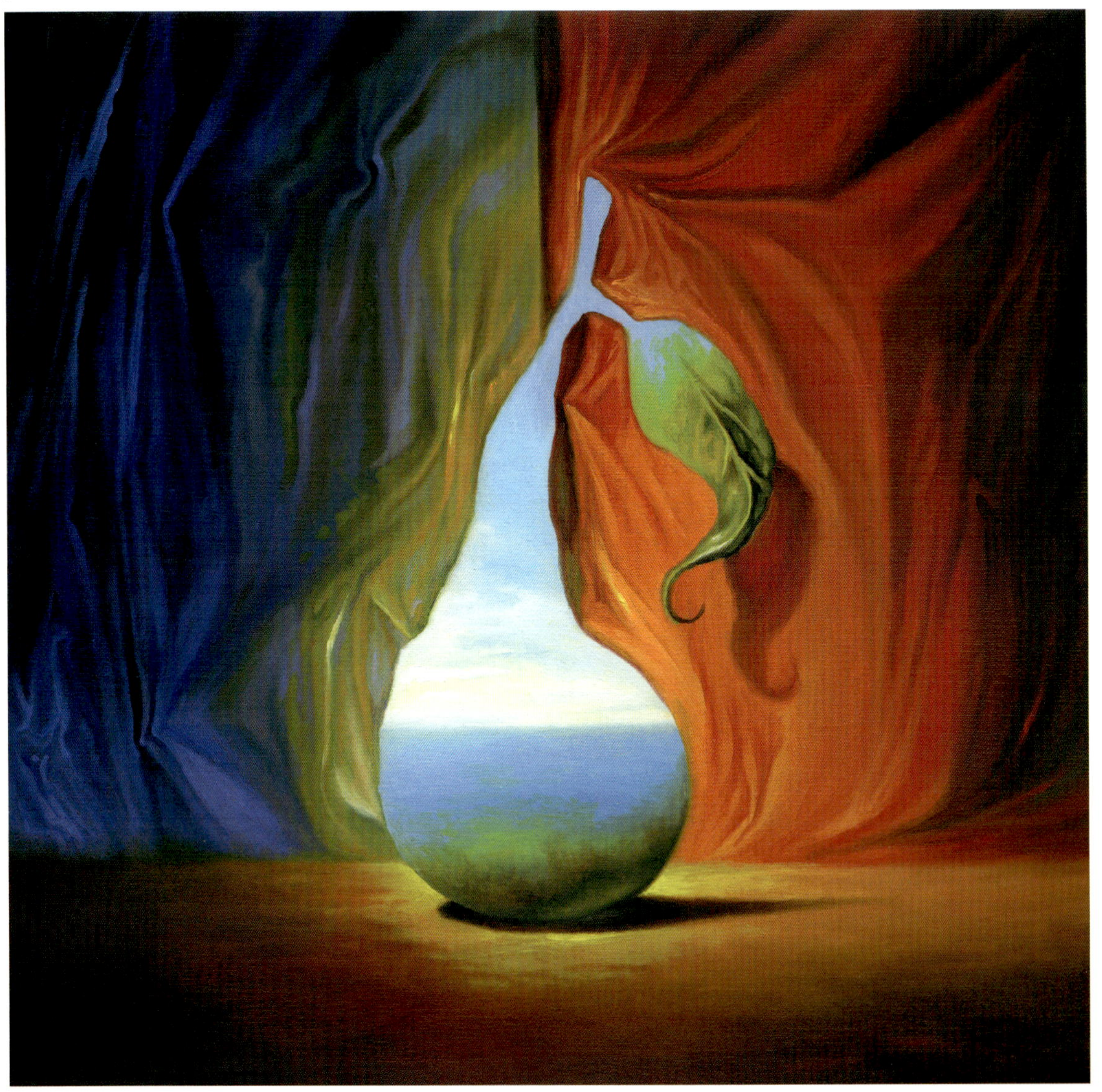

Poire de lumière · *oil on canvas*

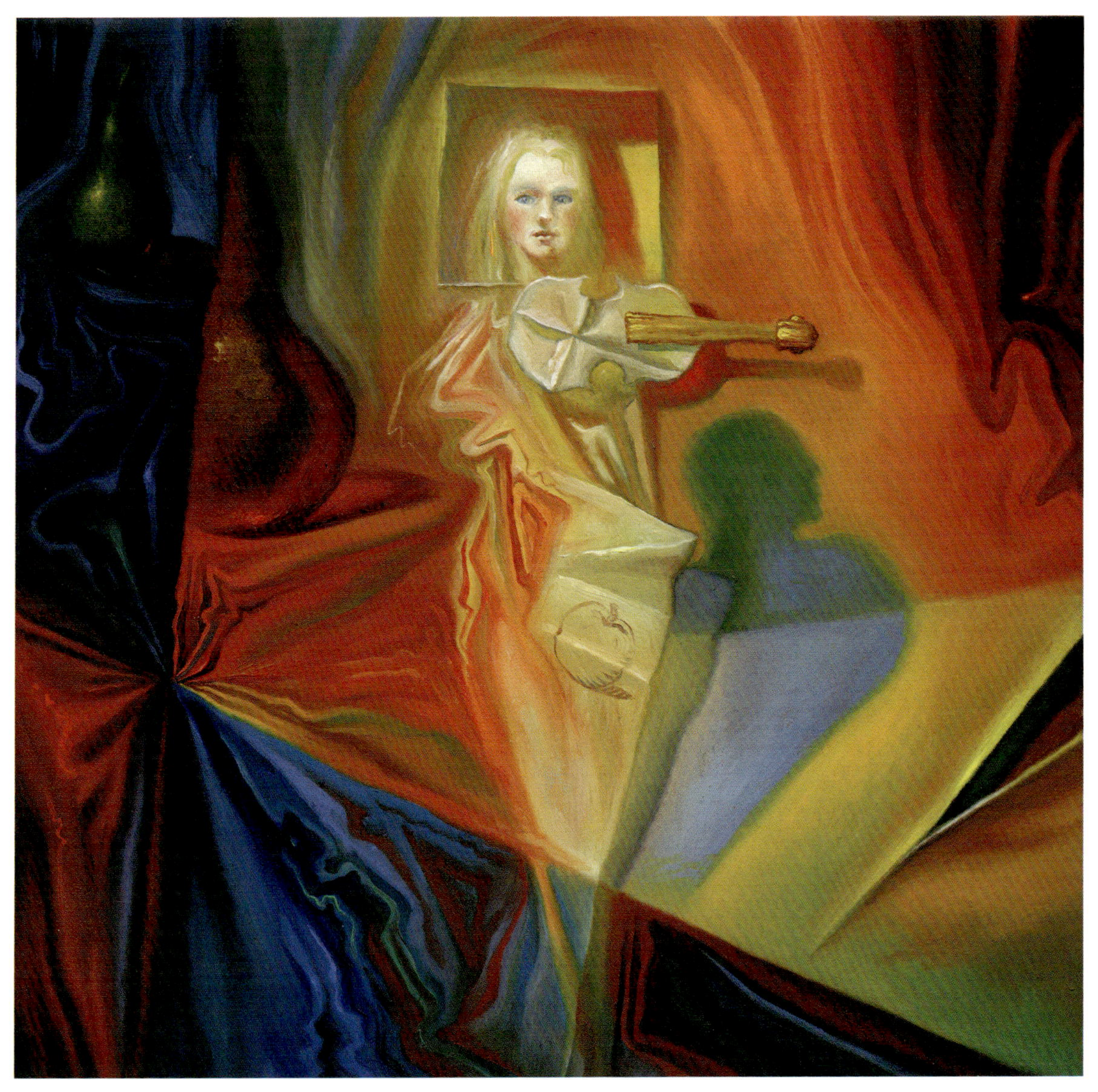

Femme avec violon · *oil on canvas*

David Stoupakis · USA

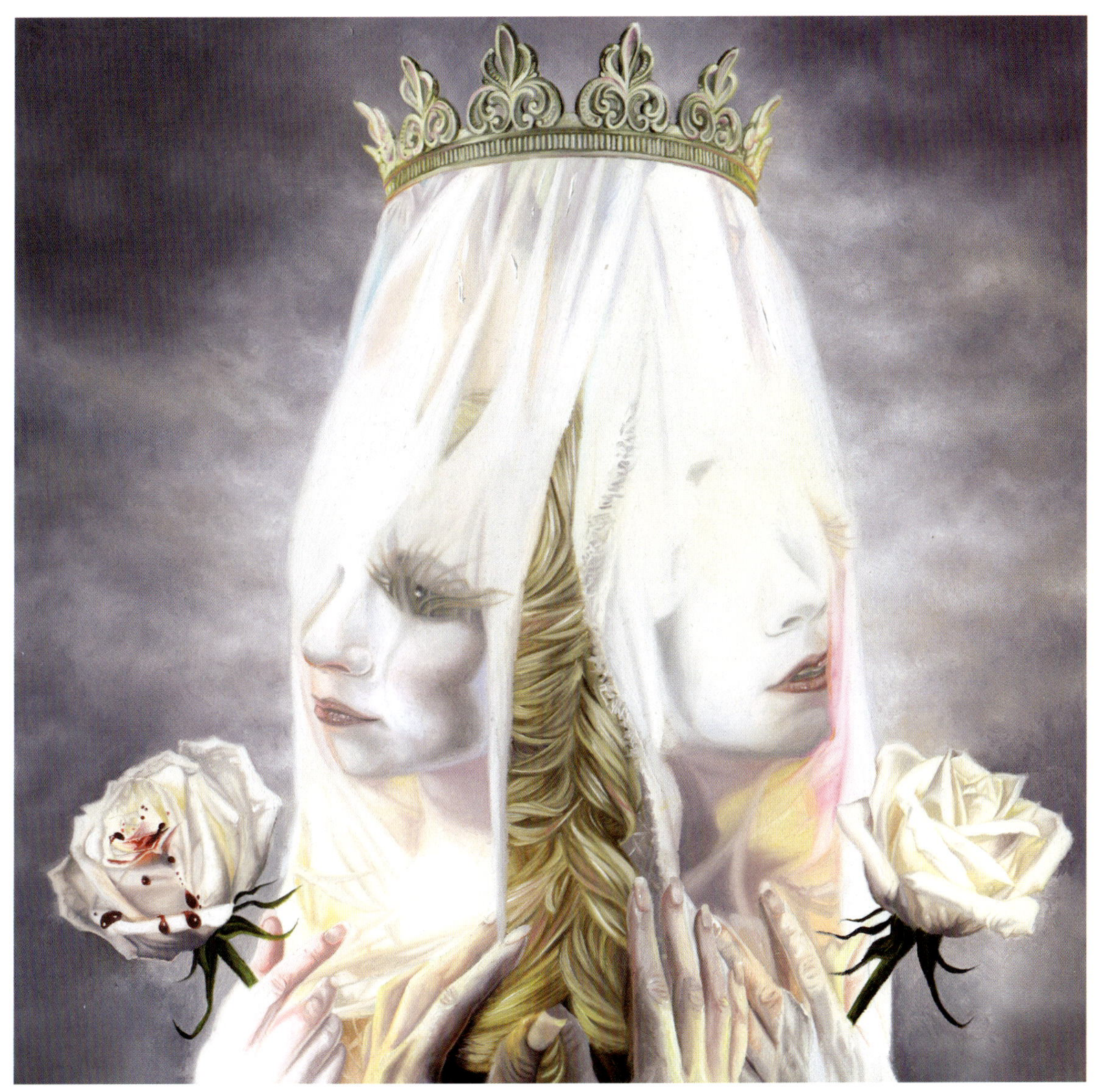

Enemy of one · *oil on panel*

Carsten Svennson · Denmark

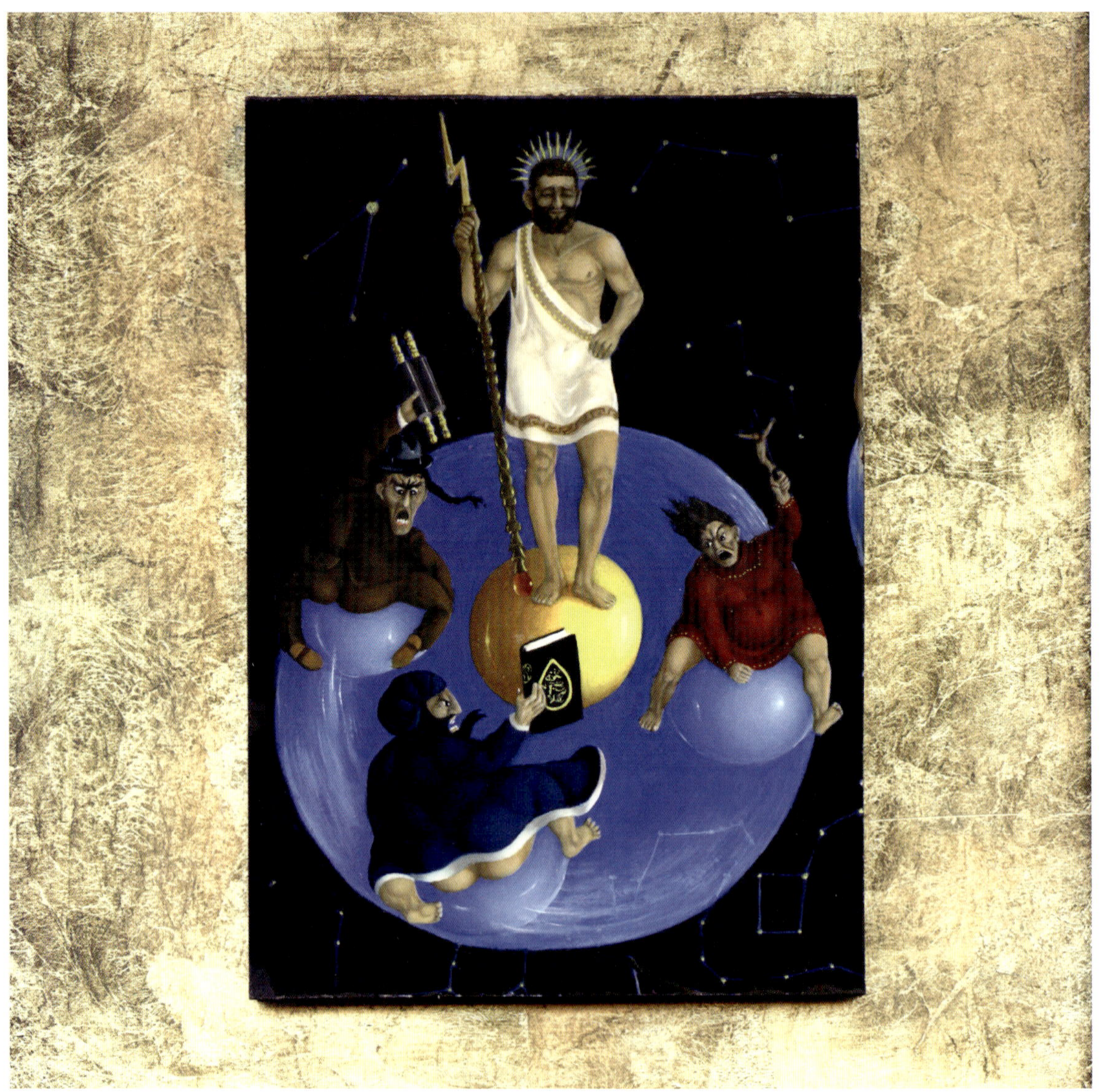

Planet of the imbacil · oil/tempera/gold on panel

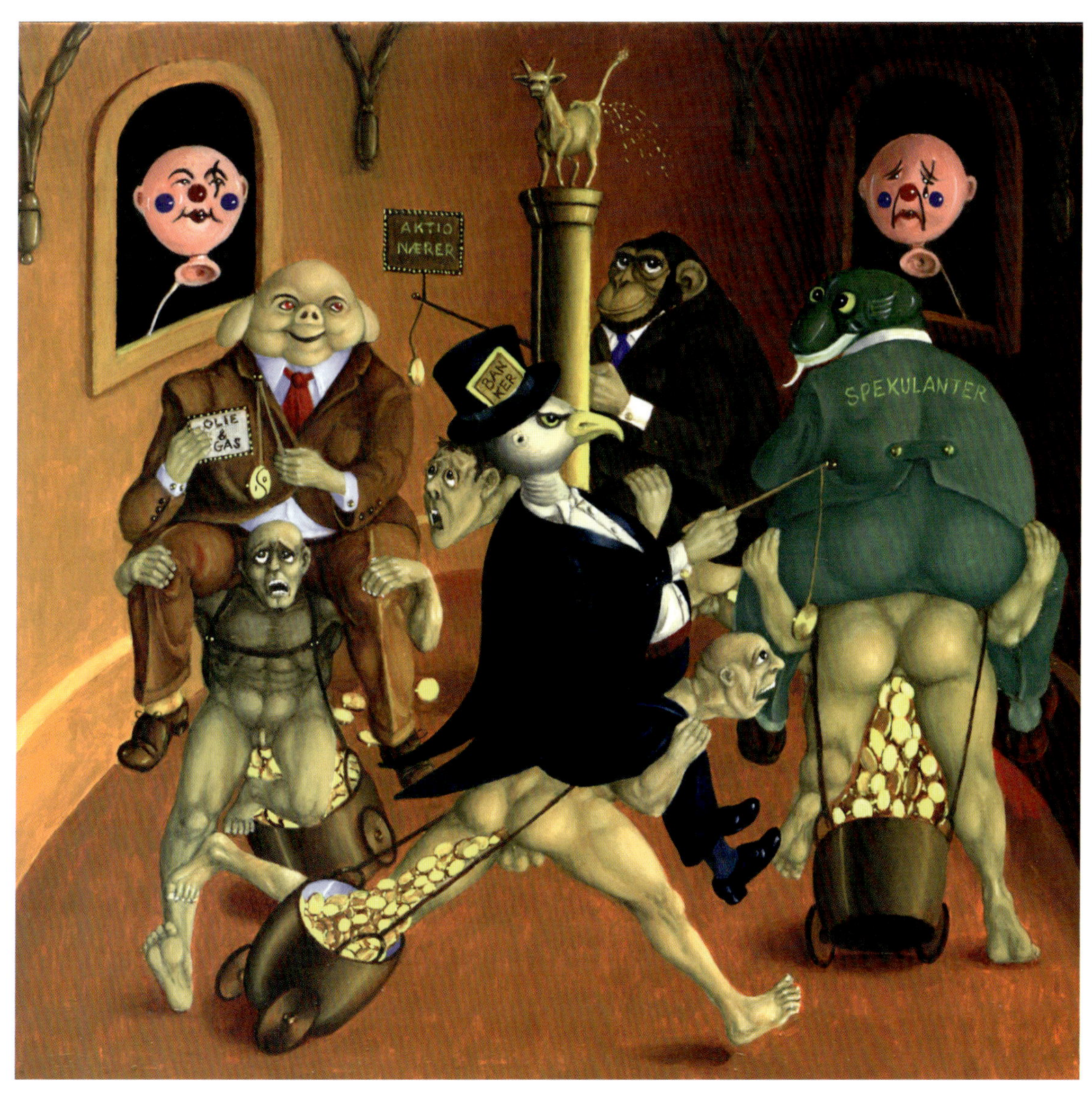

Lets dance · oil/tempera/ on panel

Yu Sugawara · Japan

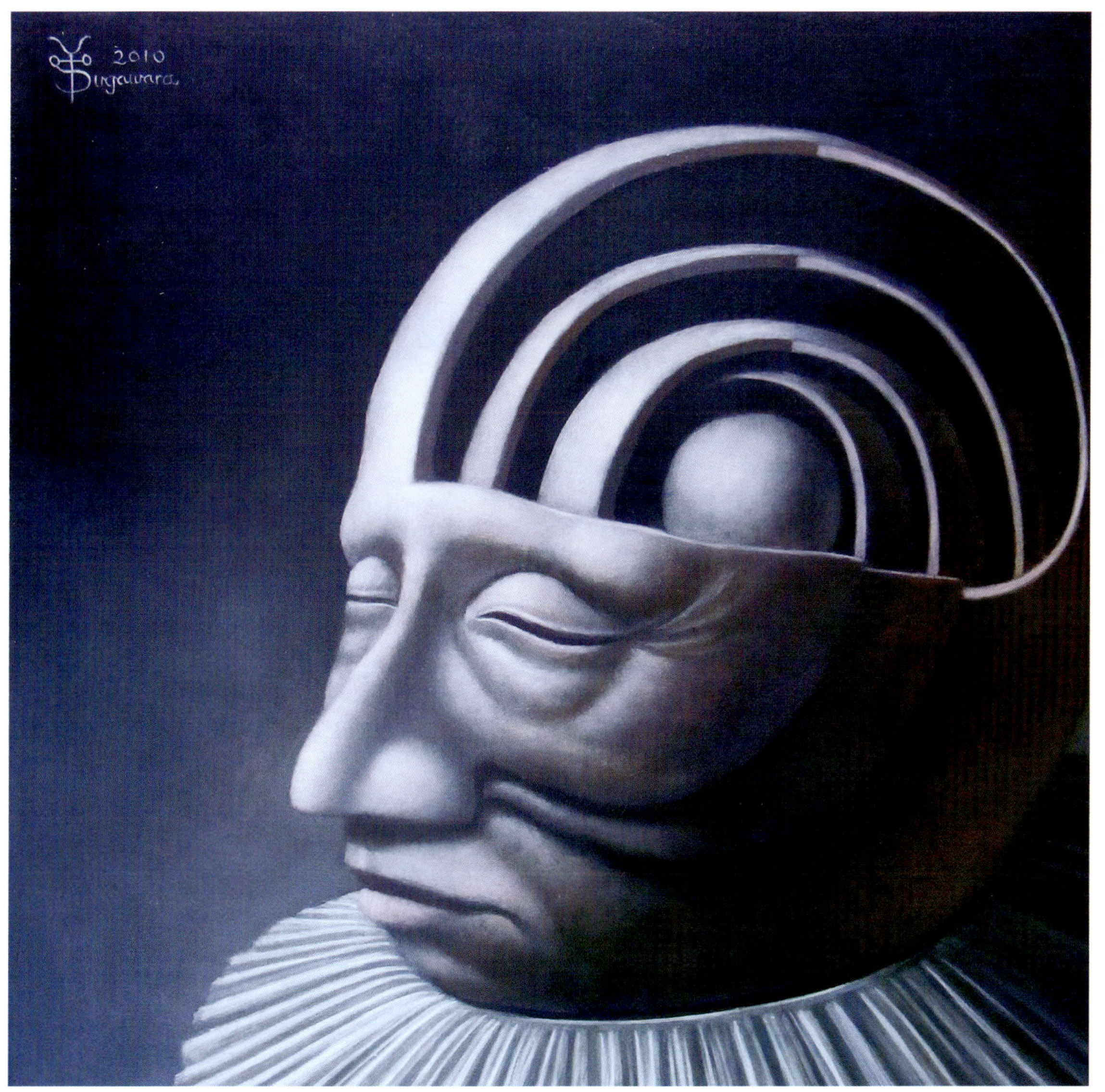

Prince of the Death · *oil on panel*

Daniël van Nes · Netherlands

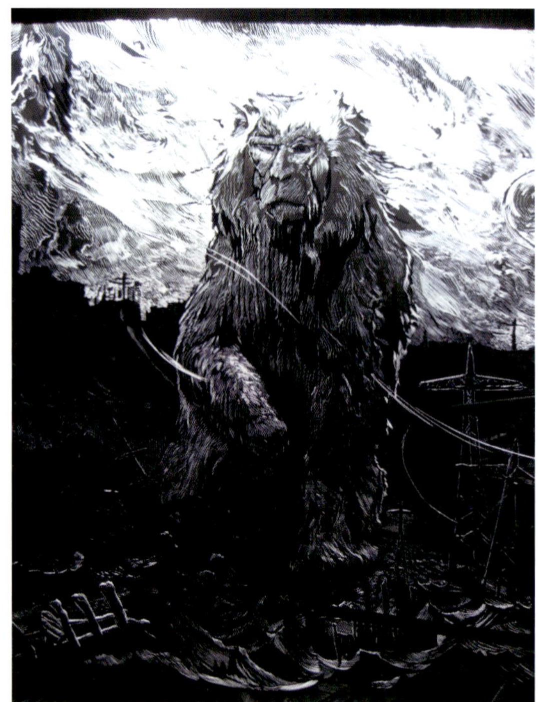

Details

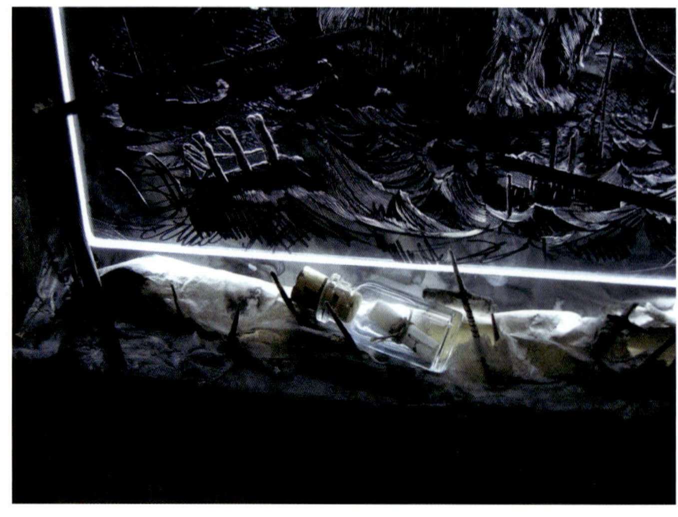

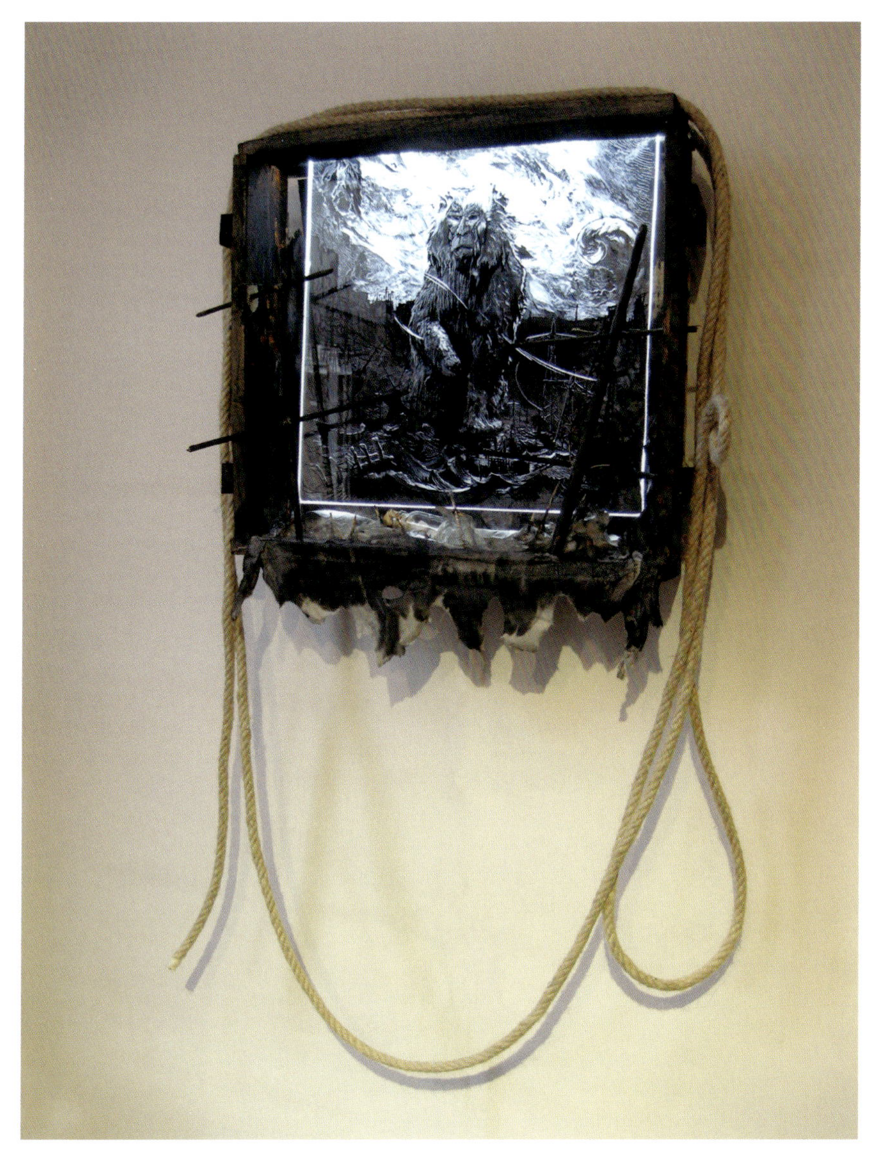

Shipwreck Carousel · *illuminated engraving & mixed media*

Raf Veulemans · Belgium

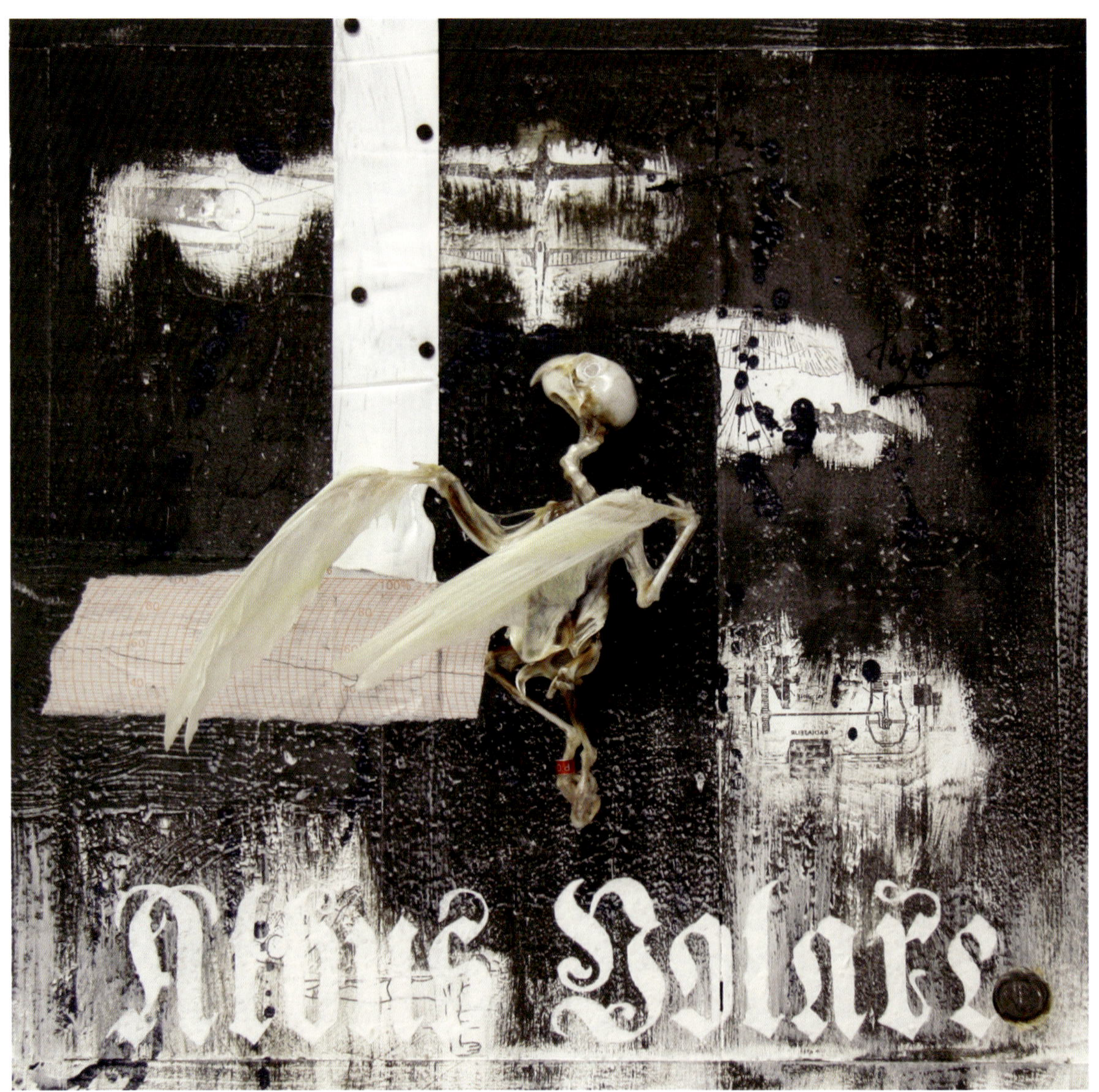

Albus Volare · *mixed media*

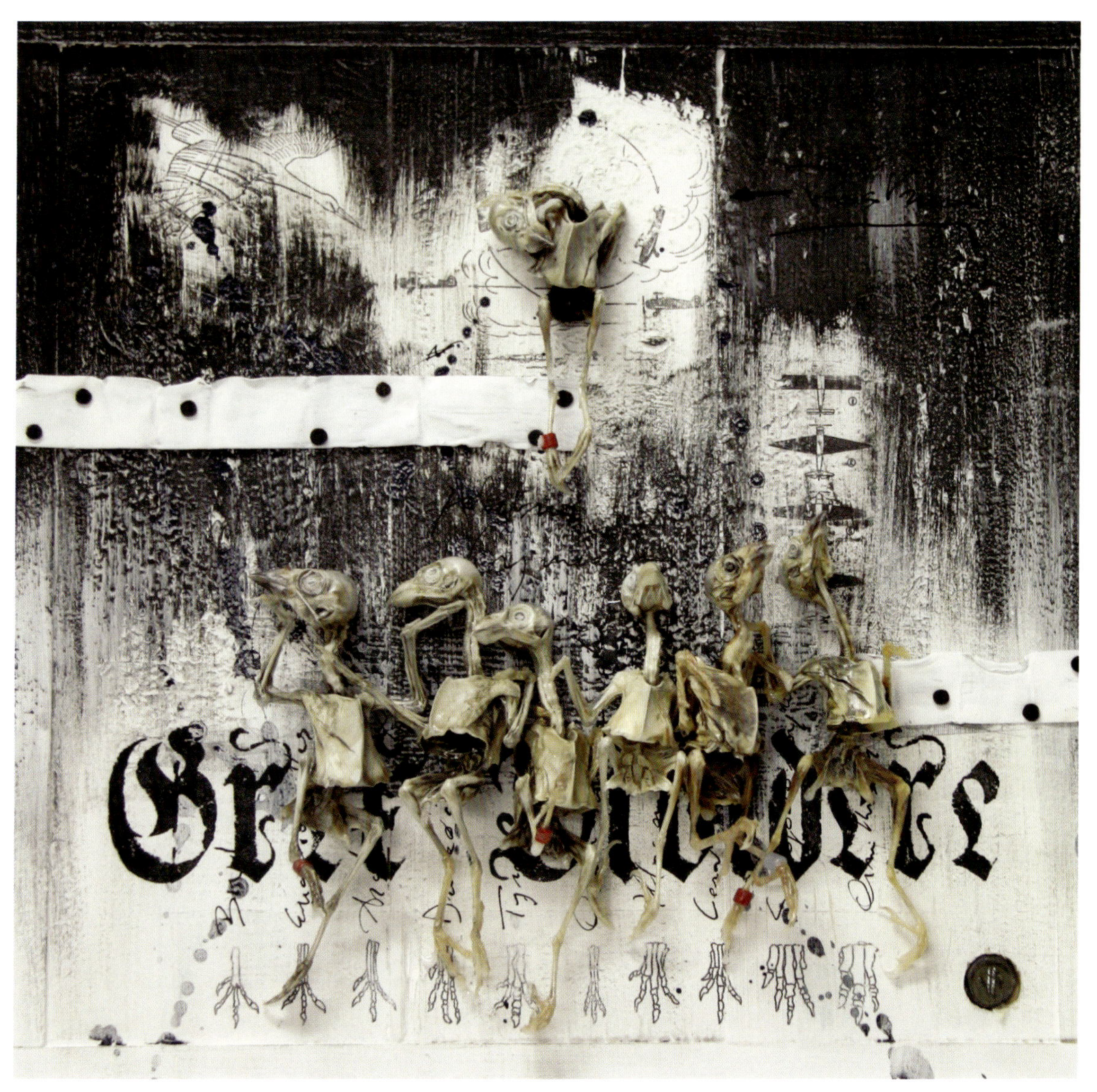

Grex dividere · *mixed media*

Cas Waterman · Netherlands

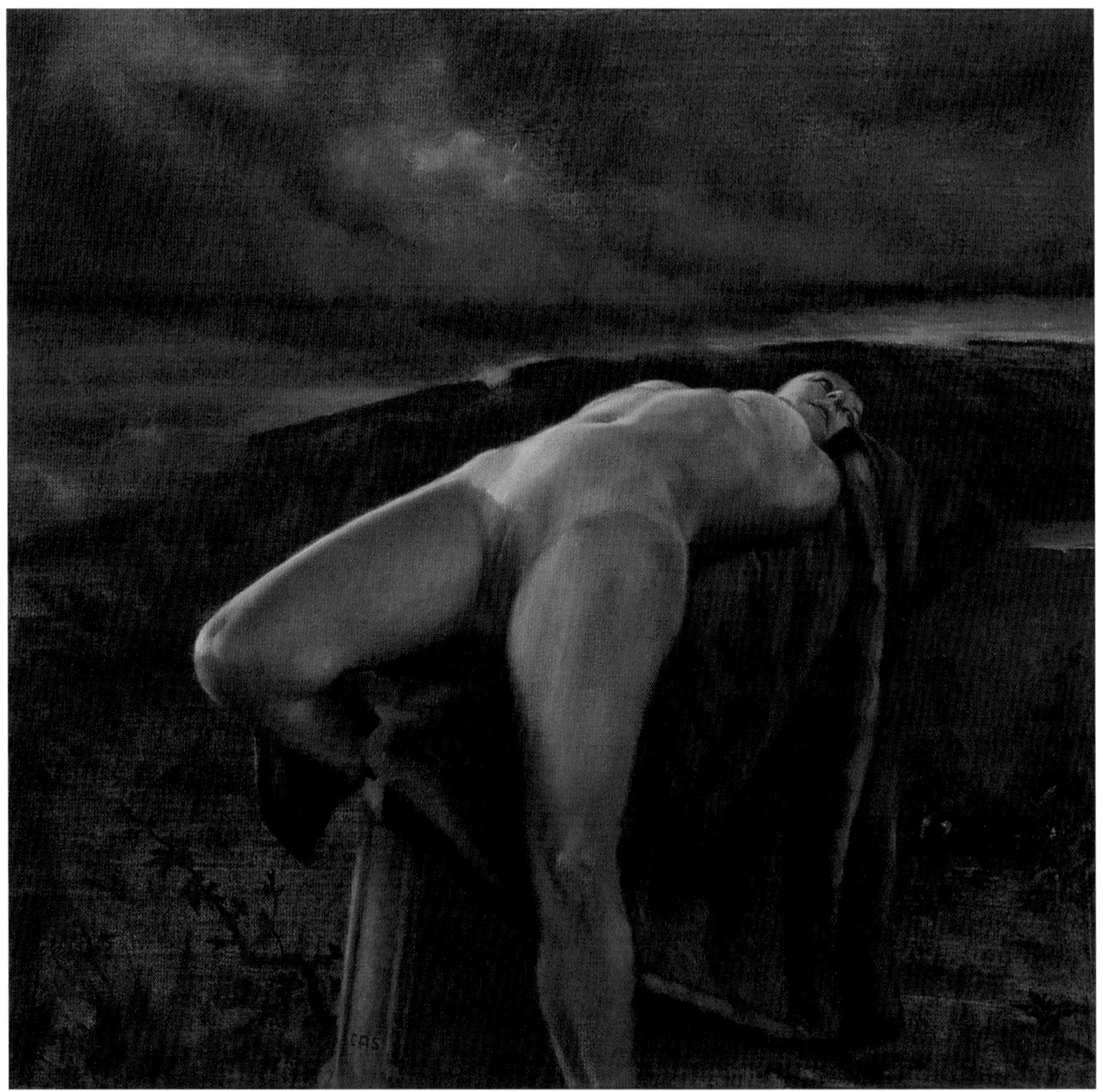

Plague stone · *oil on canvas*

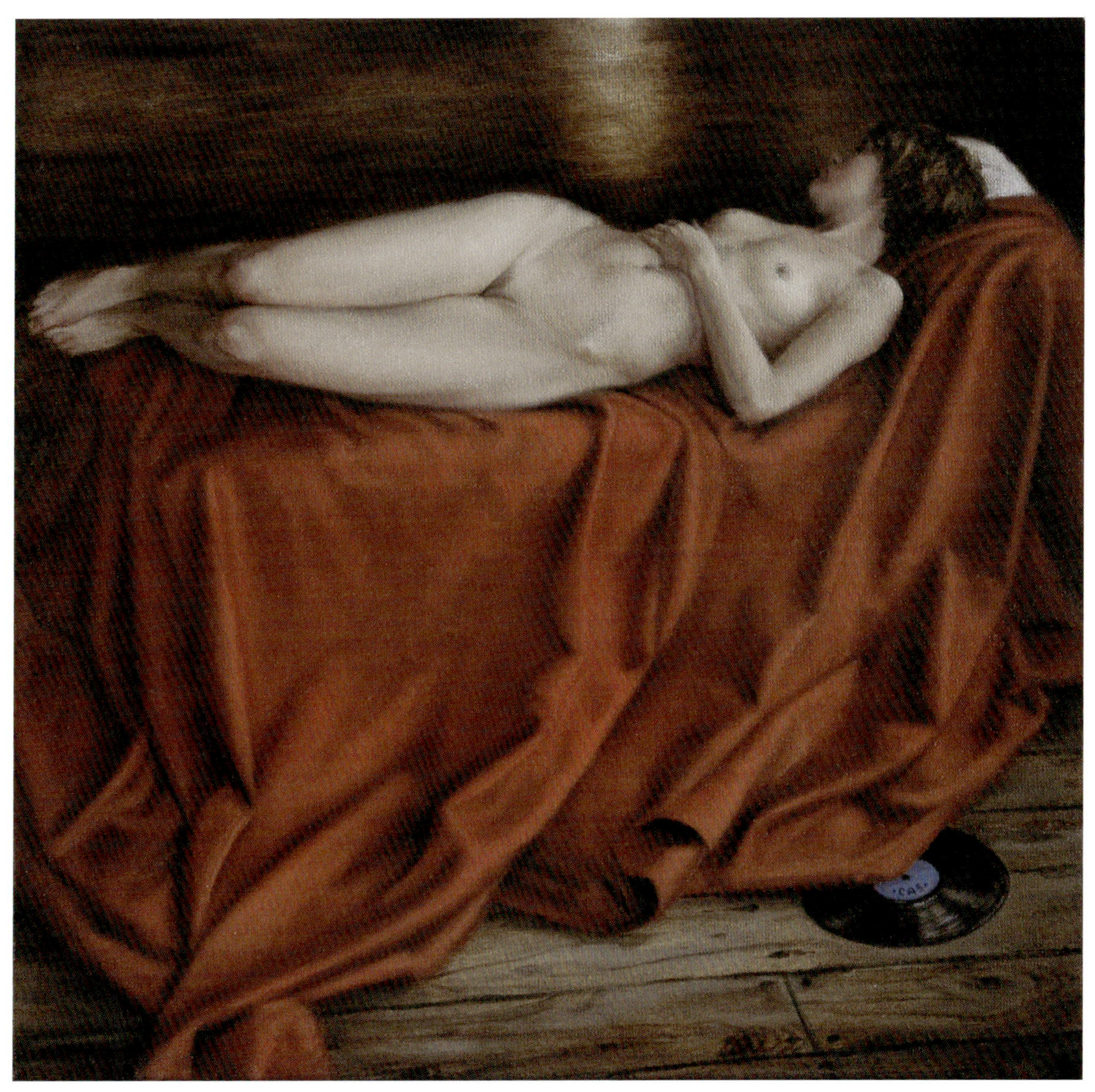

Song of the Siren · *oil on canvas*

Cliff Wallace · England

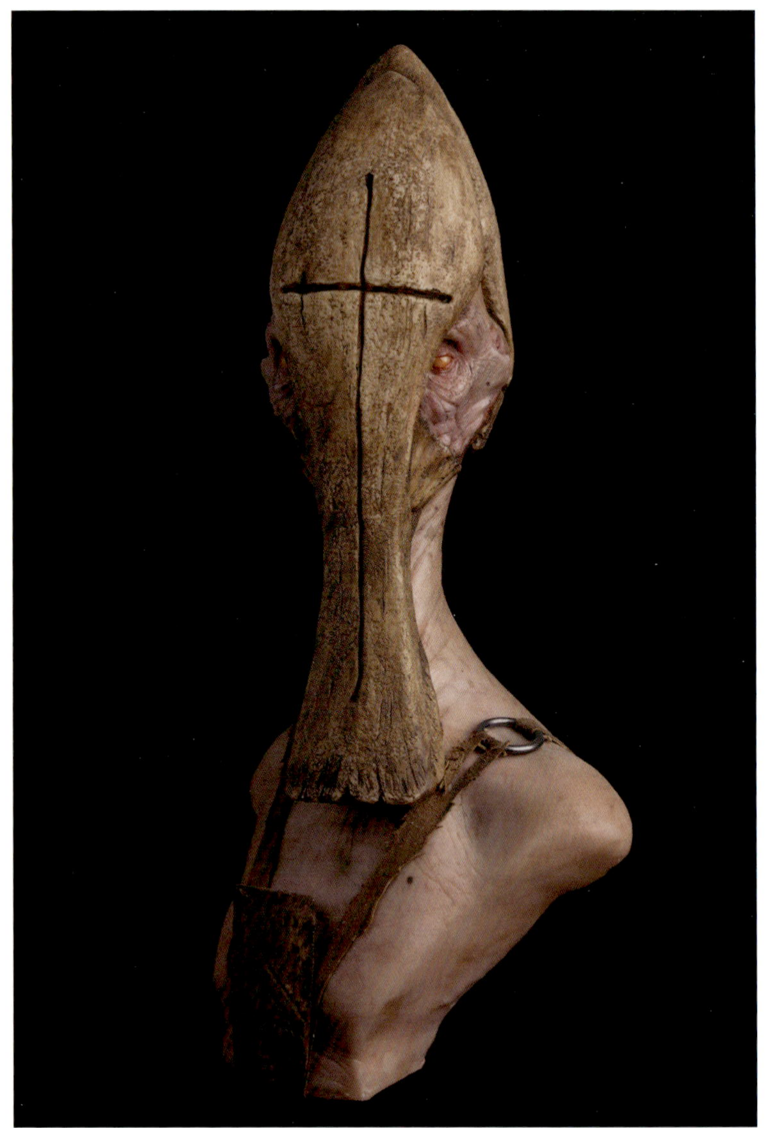

The Patriarch of Acre · *mixed media sculpture*

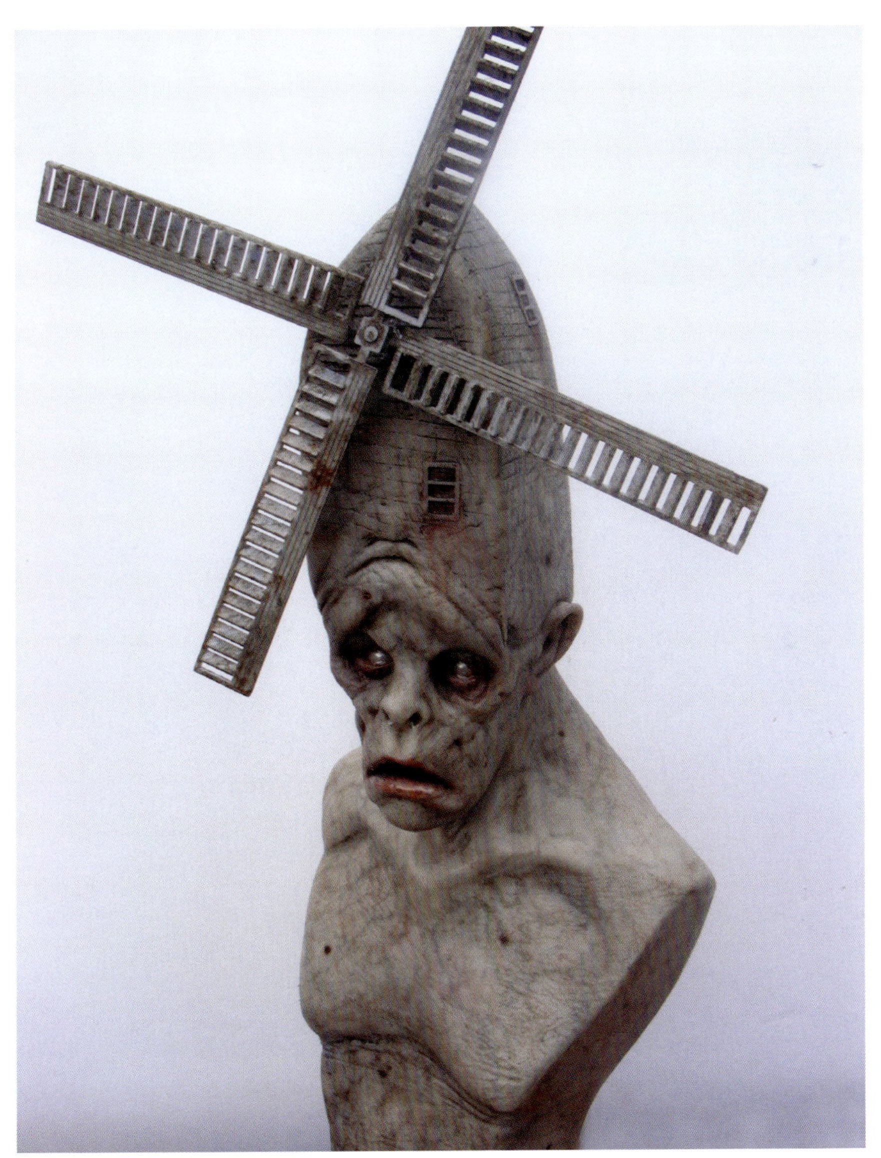

The Miller · *mixed media sculpture*

Mark Wilkinson · England

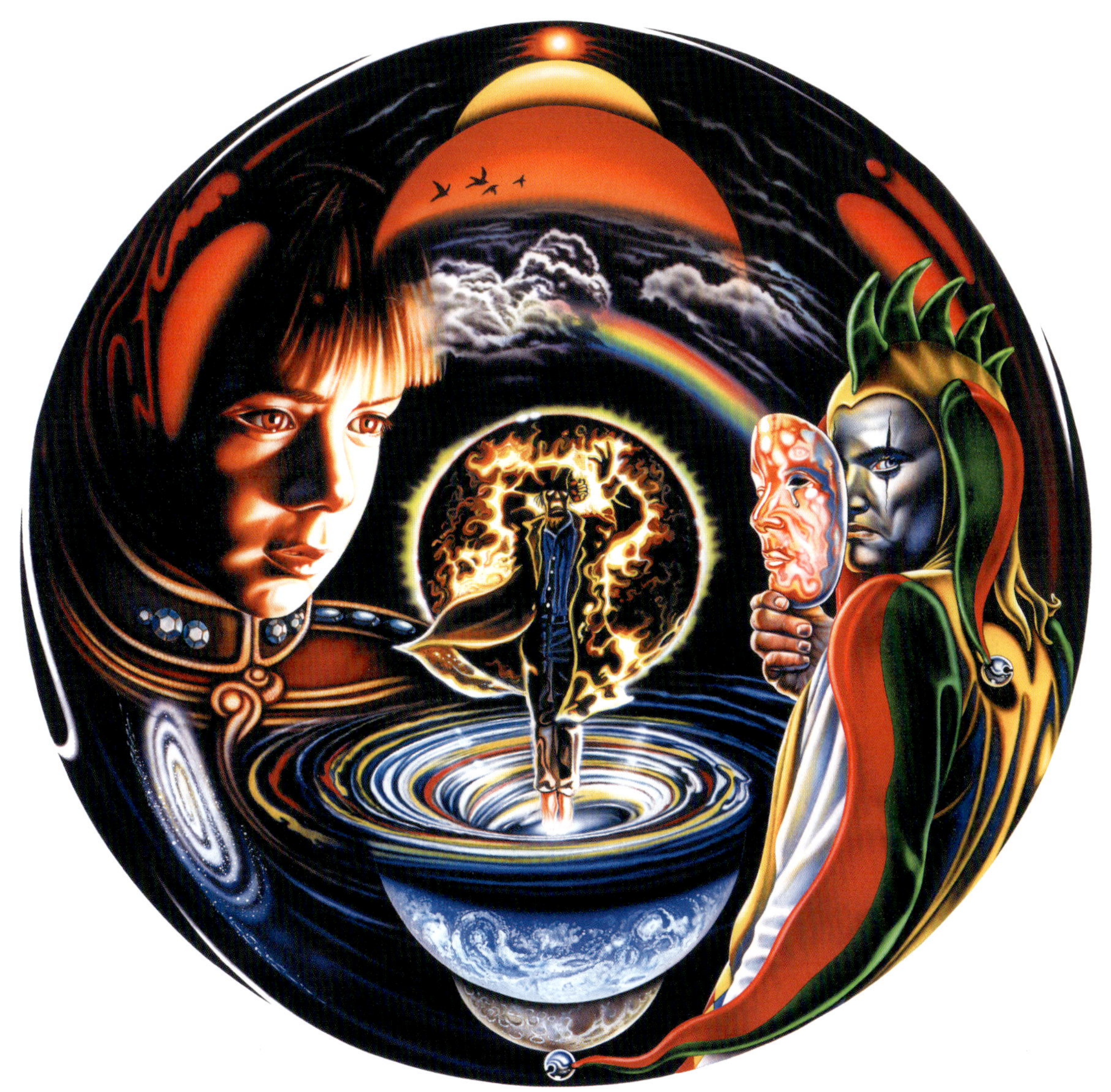

Best of Both worlds · *Airbrush and ink*

Patrick Woodroffe · England

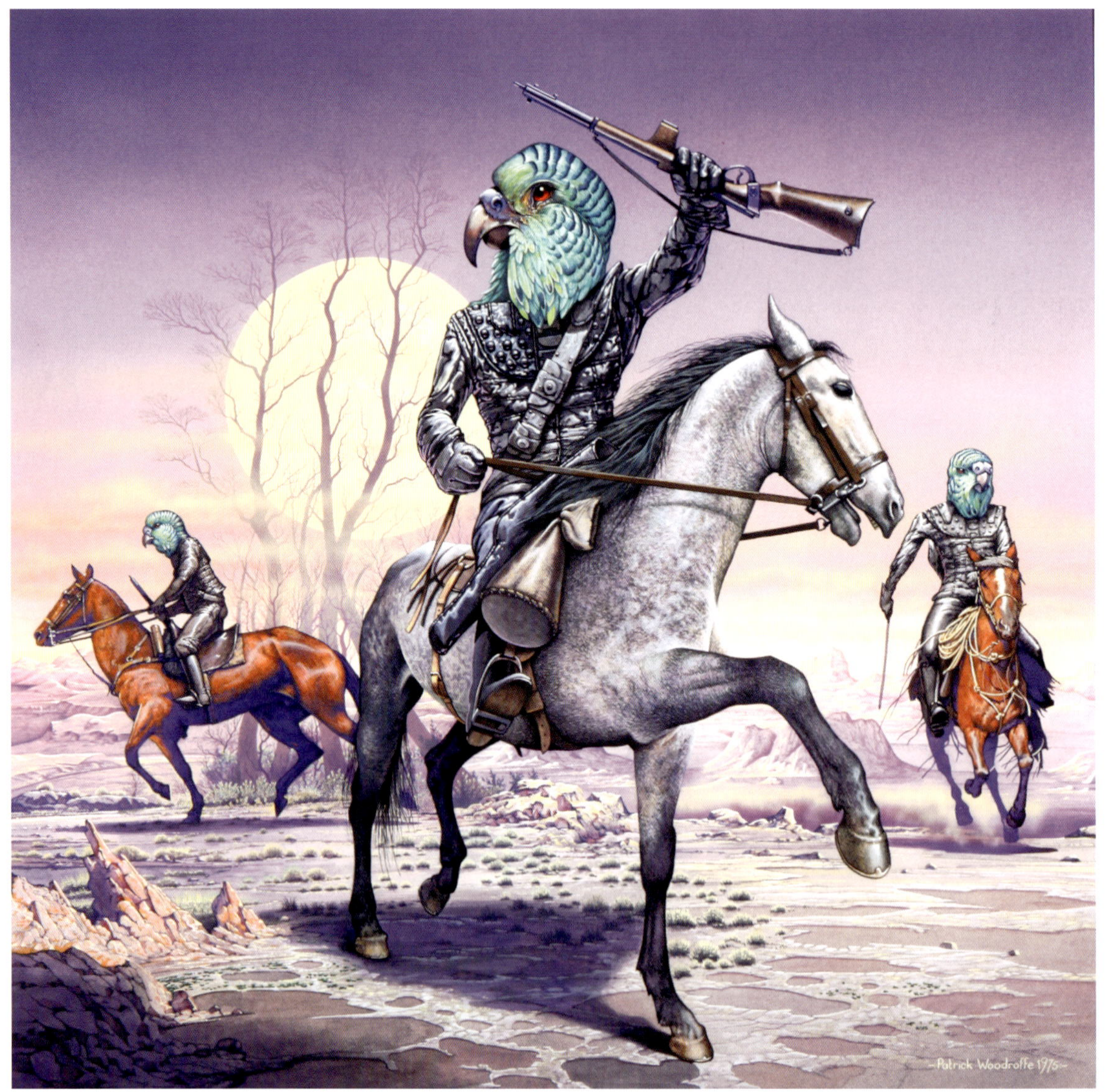

Budgie - Bandolier · *watercolour/gouach/ink on paper*

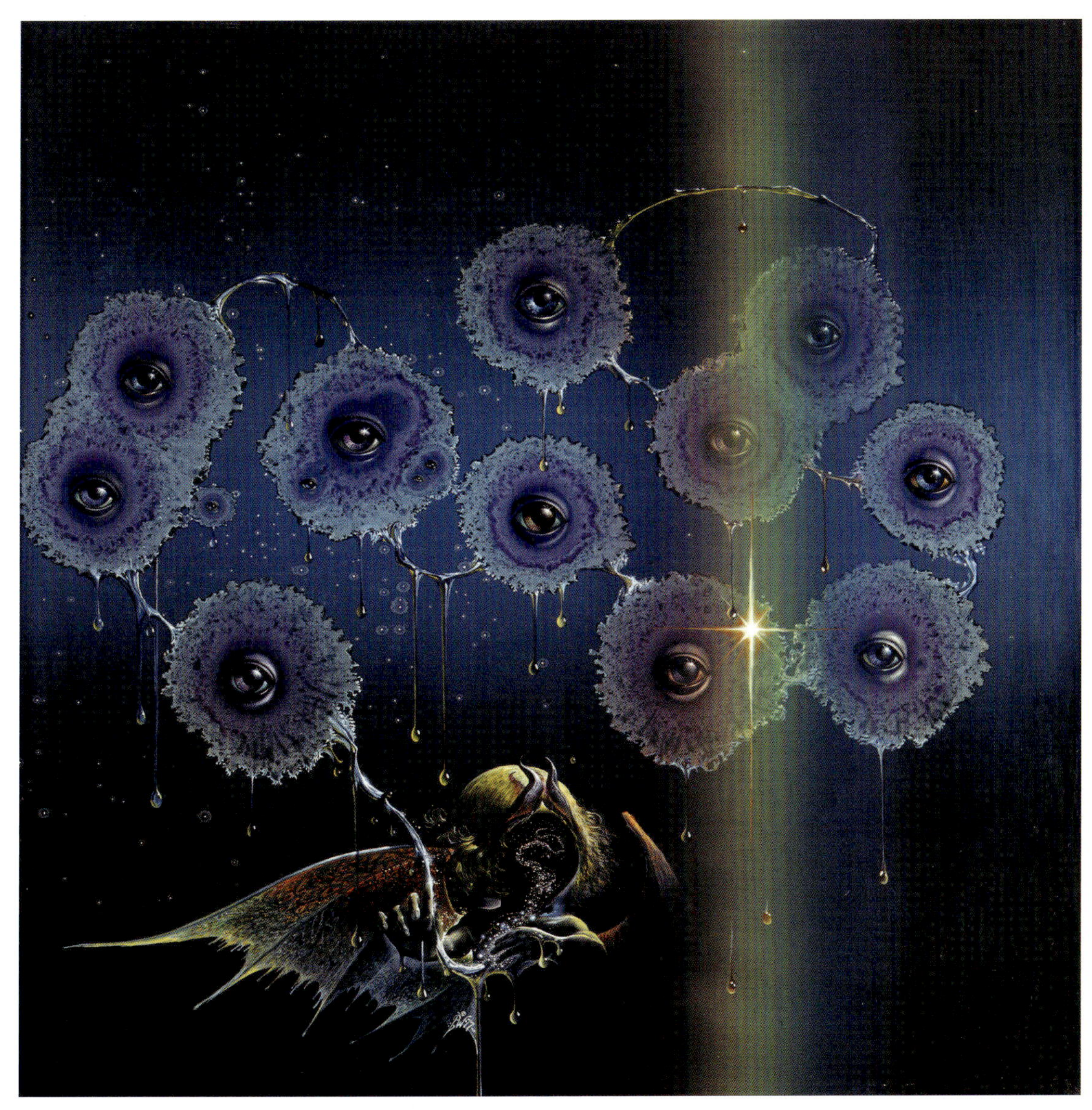

The Creation of the First Stars · *oil on panel*

Rodney Wood · USA

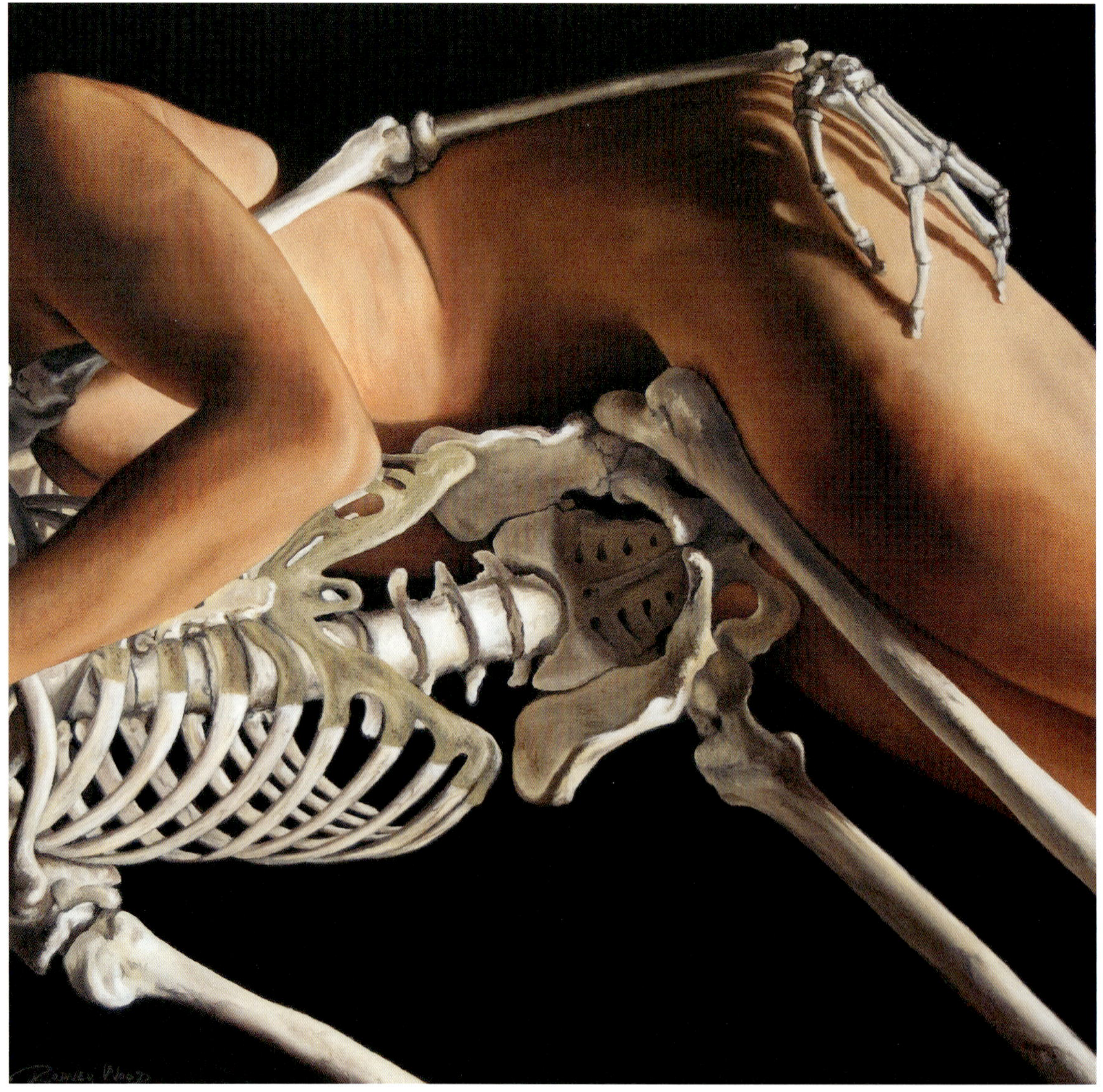

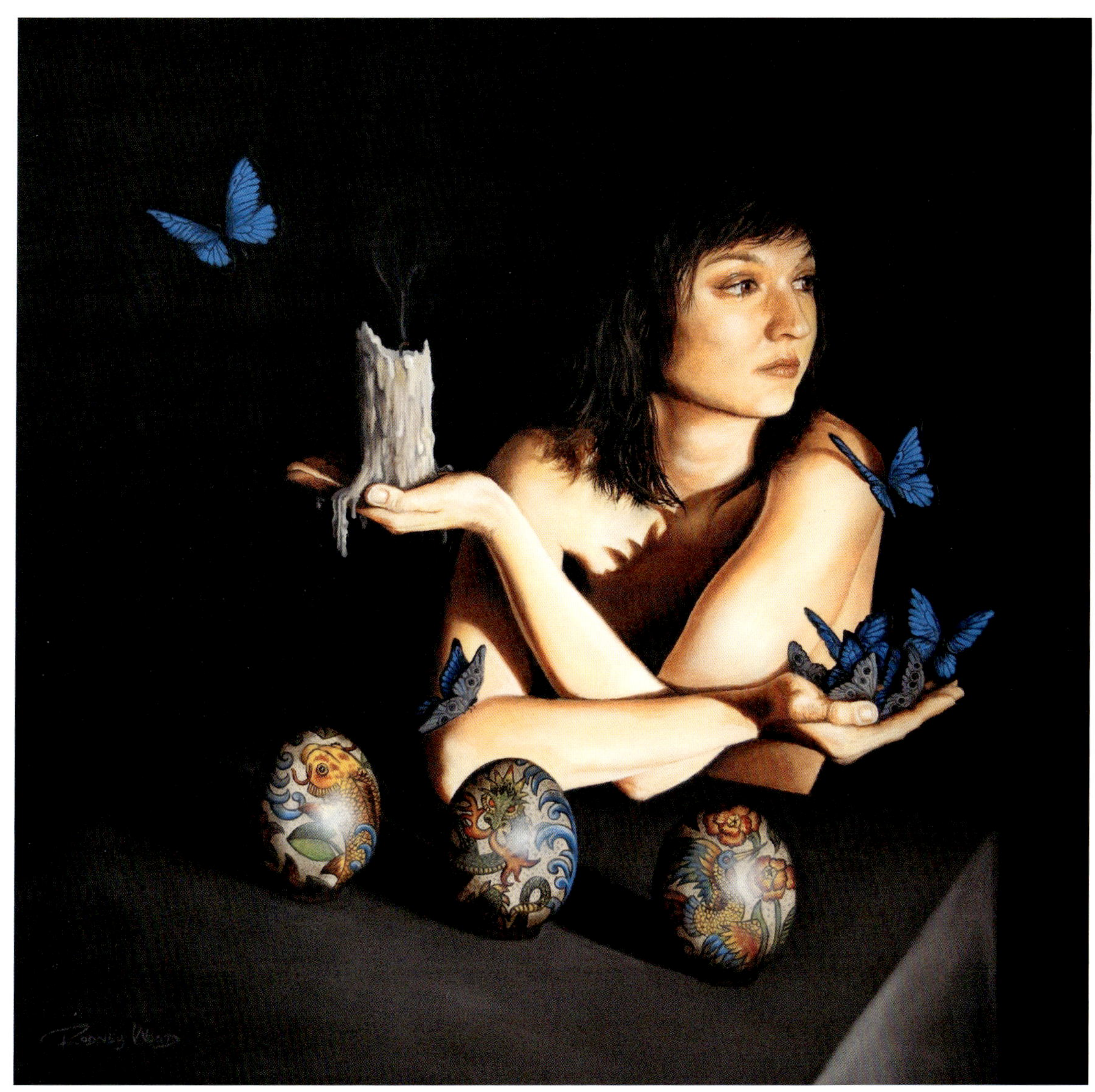

Olivier Zappelli · Switzerland

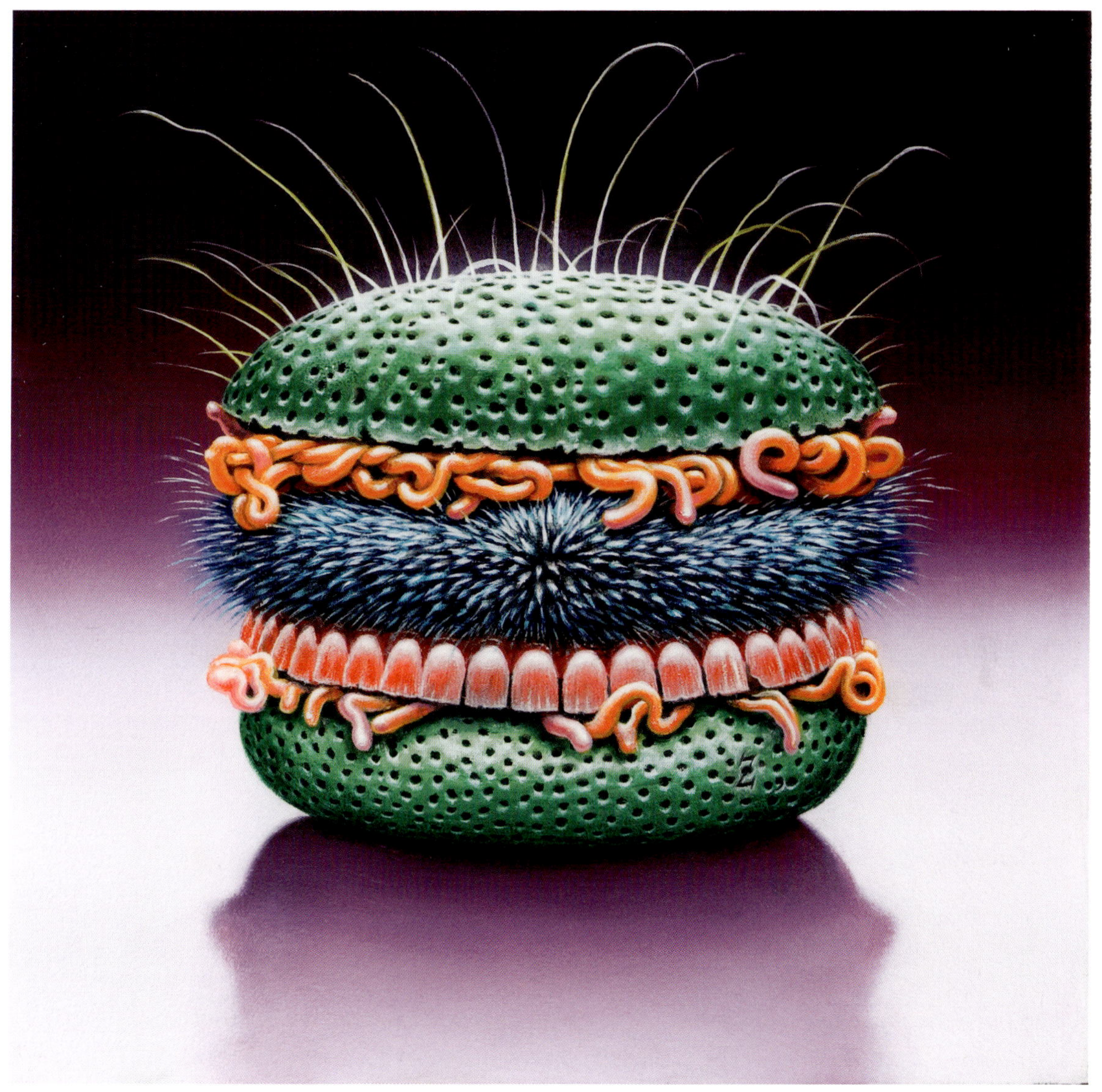

Alive Hamburger · *oil on panel*

Chet Zar · USA

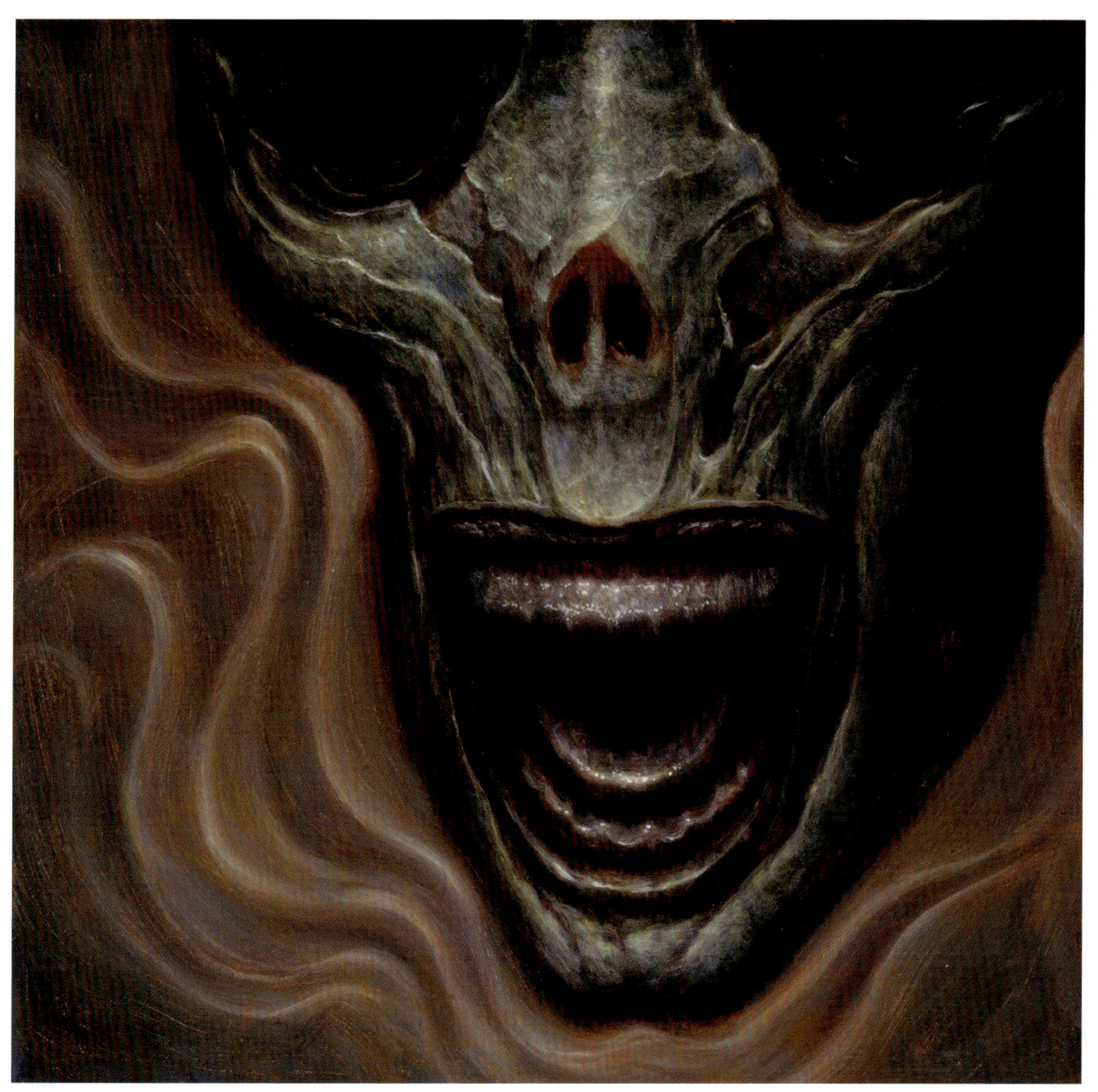

Gums of Doom · *oil on panel*

QUADRANT FANTASY

Published in Denmark 2010

QUADRANT FANTASY.
2010, with reg.
ISBN: 978-87-992147-4-7
EAN: 9788799214747

Introduction by Claus Brusen

Set in Garamond Premier Pro
Design and Layout by Dickhead Design, Denmark
Prepress and Printing by Scanprint Aarhus

Published and distributed in Europe by
FANTASMUS-ART

Distributed in North America by SCB-Distributors

Images on front cover from top left by:
Chet Zar, Michael Hiep, David Stoupakis & David M. Bowers